DID YOU KNOW THESE FASCINATING FACTS ABOUT THE LIVES, LOVES, AND CAREERS OF COUNTRY MUSIC'S GALS WITH GUITARS?

REBA MCENTIRE earned a nickel in her singing debut in a 1960 Rodeo . . . at the age of five.

After the failure "Can't Stop Myself From Loving You," DOLLY PARTON advised PATTY LOVELESS to fire her manager, who was her own brother.

THE JUDDS—mom as Vamp, daughter as Voice—won Grammy Awards in the category of Best Country Performance By A Duo Or Group With Vocal . . . in five different years.

While working in publicity for Mary Tyler Moore's record label, TRISHA YEARWOOD launched her singing career moonlighting on songwriters' demo tapes.

Thirteen year old LORRIE MORGAN'S rendition of "Paper Roses" brought her father, singing star George Morgan, to tears when he first took her to the Grand Ole Opry.

After graduating from Brown University, MARY-CHAPIN CARPENTER conquered a drinking problem and acute shyness to win a Columbia Records deal in 1987 with *HomeTown Girl*.

READ *COUNTRY GALS* AND LEARN THE TRUTH ABOUT THESE INCREDIBLE WOMEN'S HEARTBREAKS AND TRIUMPHS!

COUNTRY GALS

MARK BEGO

PINNACLE BOOKS
WINDSOR PUBLISHING CORP.

The author would like to thank the following people for their help and assistance:

Mary Bego
Bill Casey
The Country Music Association
Brad DeMeulenaere
Paul Dinas
Laura Gabriel
Randy Johnson
Barbara Jonckers
Geri Lehman
Sue "Muffy" McDonald
Marie Nemerguth
George Plentzas
David Salidor
Tony Seidl

To my Tucson "Country Gals":

Geri Lehman
Laura Gabriel
Marie Nemerguth
Melissa Porter

TABLE OF CONTENTS

EDITOR'S NOTE:

In the text of this book, there are several figures and statistics with regard to record album and single chart positions. Unless otherwise noted, they refer to the "Country Singles" and "Country Albums" charts in *Billboard* magazine.

With regard to the terms "Gold," "Platinum," "Double Platinum" etc., the following sales figures apply, as regulated by the R.I.A.A. (Record Industry Association of America):

"Gold" single = 500,000 units sold
"Platinum" single = 1,000,000 units sold
"Gold" album = 500,000 units sold
"Platinum" album = 1,000,000 units sold
"Double Platinum" album = 2,000,000 units sold
"Triple Platinum" album = 3,000,000 units sold
"Quadruple Platinum" album = 4,000,000 units sold

Introduction
Country Gals

The women in country music are no doubt one of the most creative, exciting, happening forces in the industry. In terms of sheer numbers, dollars, clout, artistry, contemporary savvy, and self-assured sexuality—they are the "Country Gals" of the 1990s—and they are bigger, better and more electrifying than ever before.

In the mid-seventies and mid-eighties, women who sang country music were epitomized by glitter and denim-decked dolls in bouffant hair-dos. They always seemed to be singing sad songs about their cheatin', drinkin', two-timin' men that done them wrong. Well, times have changed dramatically. Although one of the "Country Gals" in this book is a bona fide coal miner's daughter (Patty Loveless), she is the exception rather than the rule. They came to Nashville from a shack in the mountains (Dolly Parton), a college in the Midwest (Suzy Bogguss), a farm in Canada (k. d. lang), a trailer in Arizona (Tanya Tucker), Southern suburbia (Shelby Lynne), the nation's capital (Mary-Chapin Carpenter), and even via the Broadway stage (K. T. Oslin). Their daddies are just as likely to be prominent bankers

(Trisha Yearwood), as they are to be rodeo riders (Reba McEntire), singers at the Grand Ole Opry (Lorrie Morgan), or million-selling country music legends (Pam Tillis, Charlene Carter).

Several of these songbirds are masterful songwriters in their own right (Dolly Parton, Mary-Chapin Carpenter, K. T. Oslin, k. d. lang), and are able to make us think not only about life and love, but of the state of affairs of the world around us. While they are often labeled "new traditionalists," their musical influences are as likely to be from the songbooks of Journey (Lorrie Morgan), Elvis Presley (Trisha Yearwood), The Eagles (Tanya Tucker), Jerry Lee Lewis (Dolly Parton), Aretha Franklin (Reba McEntire), or The Dire Straits (Mary-Chapin Carpenter), as they are from Nashville songwriters.

Country music in the last decade of the twentieth century is no longer a one-note affair. Lyrically it runs the gamut from A to Z, and musically it borrows from every possible idiom that exists. Mary-Chapin Carpenter, Suzy Bogguss and Kathy Mattea have as strong a folk base as they have traditional country influences. They have more in common with Joan Baez than they do with Tammy Wynette. Trisha Yearwood and Wynonna Judd are a little bit country—and a whole lot of rock & roll. Reba McEntire and Tanya Tucker both deliver the Las Vegas glitz in their stage shows, while Shelby Lynne has taken the jazzy sound to Texas swing music and given it a new updated twist. Some of these women are happily based in country music (Patty Loveless) — while others clearly have their eyes focused on a bigger piece of the pie in the rock and pop realms (k. d. lang and K. T. Oslin). Individually and collectively, they are breaking down barriers, opening doors, shattering stereotypes and creating legendary legacies all their own.

Today's women in the country music spotlight have long since come out of the kitchen and resolutely stood up for their convictions — via their music and through their actions. They're not wasting their time by lounging on the veranda planning country picnics. They're organizing AIDS fundraisers and awareness campaigns (Kathy Mattea and Mary-Chapin Carpenter), singing to save the environment (Trisha Yearwood), standing up for animal and human rights (k. d. lang), promoting self-awareness (K. T. Oslin), and looking to find answers to make this a better world (Dolly Parton).

The ladies of country music have been around as long as the genre has existed. It was the early 1900s when hoe-down down-home Ozark mountain folk music was labeled "country." Since it came out of a religious, "family values" kind of an atmosphere, the first "Country Gals" were epitomized by family singing units like The Carter Family, and that trio's star, "Mother Maybelle" Carter. Speaking of her famous grandmother Maybelle, Carlene Carter recalls, "The thing I remember the most is: she had a wonderful sense of humor and she loved what she did so much — it was *real* folk music at its best."

There were no country showgirls in the 1930s and 1940s, but there were several singing cowgirls. Patsy Montana, whose thirties smash "I Want to Be a Cowboy's Sweetheart" brought the Western swing down home on the range. In the forties, glamorous Dale Evans was the perfect boots-and-fringe bedazzled cinematic counterpart to Roy Rogers, the singing cowboy who captured her heart on and off the screen.

The 1950s had Kitty Wells ("Jealousy") and Patti Paige ("Allegheny Moon"), who both melded country songs with pop appeal. However, in the late fifties and early sixties came the undisputed all-time high priestess of country music — Patsy Cline.

A bawdy, searing, passionate singer — Cline to this day is revered as the idol of idols of the majority of the women in this book. Patsy's sometimes boisterous, sometimes heart-wrenching vocals are as timelessly touching in the 1990s as they were four decades ago. From the raucous rockabilly sound of "Honky Tonk Merry-Go-Round," to her pop interpretations of "Love Letters in the Sand," to her brilliant country signature songs "Sweet Dreams" and "Crazy," Patsy Cline's music still has an emotional poignancy that cuts through to the heart, for her listeners and fans. Over thirty years since her death in a tragic plane crash, through her recordings she maintains her appeal and her mystique.

"Probably the woman who embodied the Nashville sound more than anyone is Patsy Cline — *absolutely*," says Kathy Mattea. Likewise, K. T.

Oslin proclaims, "You believed what she sang. You believed what she was talking about. She had a style that was all her own, and still is."

In addition to Cline's music, it is her spunky attitude that magnifies her appeal. According to Lorrie Morgan, "I think that Patsy was probably the first strong-headed woman in country music. It was like: 'She is not gonna take nothin' off of nobody.' And, I think we all admire that in Patsy. But, there was a soft side in Patsy, too, that came out in the ballads. Which, I think we all would like people to read in us, I think the way we read Patsy."

In the mid-sixties and early seventies, it was Loretta Lynn and Tammy Wynette who were the superstar "Country Gals," along with Bobbie Gentry, Lynn Anderson, Jeannie C. Riley, and the pre-crossover Dolly Parton. However, it was in 1975 that someone else arrived on the country scene—from the most unlikely source: the world of rock & roll. The specific milestone album that did it was called "Heart Like a Wheel," and the singer was Linda Ronstadt.

Born in Tucson, Arizona, and musically educated on Hollywood's Sunset Strip, Linda had the instinct and the determination to freely blend the twang of traditional country music with a fresh rock & roll beat. Few people remember that The Eagles started out in the seventies as Linda Ronstadt's back-up band, or the fact that she hand-selected them at Los Angeles's premiere folk/rock showcase club, The Troubadour. Through Linda's mid-seventies albums (particularly "Prisoner In Disguise," "Hasten Down The Wind," and "Simple Dreams"), her predominantly rock-oriented audience suddenly found themselves exposed to the music and/or singing of Dolly Parton, Emmylou Harris, Patsy Cline, and Maria Muldaur. Although Ronstadt has subsequently gone on to become the most famous singing chameleon in the business (opera, pop standards, Cuban mambo, Mexican canciones, Gilbert & Sullivan, . . . etc.), she is the second most important influence mentioned by today's "Country Gals."

According to Ronstadt aficionado Trisha Yearwood, "The first thing that I remember about hearing Linda Ronstadt was hearing that voice. There was a power and an emotion, and she believed every single word she said. And, I had not ever heard that ever before."

Pam Tillis echoes the sentiment by proclaiming, "Emmylou Harris and Linda Ronstadt had everyone's attention. They were young women who reflected both the respect for tradition, with the rock music that was happening at the time. It made for some really great music."

Throughout this entire era, another country gal was gaining broad-based popularity. Her name— Dolly Parton. Thanks to her seventies songs "I Will Always Love You" and "Here You Come Again," she has become a huge country star. However, via her eighties and nineties film career, Parton has become one of Hollywood's biggest and most consistently exciting female singing stars. Her late eighties return to 100 percent country singing has made her a smashing 1990s "Platinum" selling country gal.

If all of the women in this book were going to form a sorority, Dolly Parton would assuredly be the group's den mother. She is the common link between the majority of the gals in this book. It was Dolly who took Patty Loveless under her wing when 14-year-old Loveless first hit Nashville. Parton has recorded with Kathy Mattea, Mary-Chapin Carpenter, Lorrie Morgan, Pam Tillis, and Tanya Tucker. Suzy Bogguss got her big break as a singer at Parton's amusement park, Dollywood. When members of Reba McEntire's band perished in a tragic plane crash, Dolly called to offer support. In addition, Parton has had the longest span of hit recordings of any of the women on these pages.

The current excitement about women in country music can be directly traced back to one particular 1987 album. It was the epitome of the "new traditionalist" sound, and it became a Grammy Award winning smash. The album was *Trio* by Linda Ronstadt, Dolly Parton and Emmylou Harris. Not only was the sound of the music comprised of uniformly stripped-down acoustic instrumentals, but it also attracted the individual fans of all three women to purchase it. Since that time, the proliferation of country gals has virtually exploded. Up until that point, it seemed that the country men dominated the charts. Well, they've had to move over to make way for a whole batch of eighties ladies since then!

Now we come to the title of this book: *Country Gals.* When the idea behind this book came about — I didn't know what to call it. I have also written a 1994 book entitled *Country Hunks* about today's hot country men. That was simple enough to title. However, *this* book presented a real dilemma. "What on Earth am I going to name it?" I asked all of my friends. "Country Songbirds?" "Country Dolls?" "Country Chicks?" "Country Flames?" "Country Sirens?" "Country Babes?" Nothing seemed to work.

My dilemma was echoed by Reba McEntire, who recently exclaimed, "I don't like to be referred to as a 'gal' or a 'chick' or a 'broad.' I think women need to be strong." Unfortunately, I didn't have Reba's phone number so that I could call her and ask her what other word she preferred!

When my book contract arrived from the publisher, I immediately noted that my tentative title "Country Songbirds" had been changed to "Country Gals." The problem was that I didn't like either title. Again I wracked my brain. In a book that runs the gamut from frilly Dolly Parton to mannish k. d. lang, to no-nonsense Mary-Chapin Carpenter, to explosive Shelby Lynne, to glittery Reba McEntire — it all seemed to defy the magical umbrella term that I sought to discover. Finally, after surveying every synonym I could think of — I finally had to concede: "Okay, *Country Gals* it is!"

Regardless of what I called them in the title of this book, the facts remain: the fifteen women in the following chapters represent the biggest, the hottest, the most popular women in 1990s country music. They are talented, evocative, sexy and savvy.

Although I was personally "into" the music of the majority of the singers in this book before assembling it, along the way I discovered some excellent music through the albums mentioned on these pages. Hopefully you will do the same thing after reading this volume.

To paraphrase the title of a women's rights song by Aretha Franklin and Annie Lennox of the Eurythmics: these fifteen "Sisters Are Doin' It For Themselves!" In addition, these "Country Gals" have a long tradition in country music to follow — from Patsy Montana and Patsy Cline, to Loretta Lynn and Tammy Wynette. As Pam Tillis so wonderfully puts it, "Women pioneered country music. They *are* country music. Boy, I just hope I'm worthy to walk a mile in their high heels!"

They're cool, contemporary, confident — and they are burning up the country-music charts like never before. They are the 1990s most exciting country gals, and the excitement's just begun!

—*Mark Bego*

January 1994

Chapter One
Reba McEntire

Reba McEntire is the epitome of the 1990s country music success story. With her feisty determination and her trademark fiery red hair, she has masterfully forged ahead to create a sizzling multimedia career. She is a bigger-than-life entertainer whose launching platform just happens to be country music.

She may be the currently reigning queen of the country music scene, but her image is one of sheer glamour and glitz. On stage her presentation is poised, her act is polished, and unfolds with precision pacing. Although she may wear jeans and boots in her personal life, in her act she shimmers in beaded and sequined gowns. There is no question that Reba McEntire is 100 percent a star, and from the minute she walks out on stage, the audience is eating out of her hand.

Unlike many of the women on top of today's country music scene, Reba's career didn't take off on the first album or two. There were thirteen years between her first album, *Reba McEntire* in 1978, and the "Double Platinum" success of 1991's *For My Broken Heart*.

Today Reba's glittering realm includes movies, videos, sold-out concerts, TV specials, magazine cover stories, and enough awards and honors to fill a trophy room. She has twelve "Gold" albums, five "Platinum" albums, and her 1992 release, *It's Your Call*, continued her "Double Platinum" streak. Her 1993 number-one duet with Vince Gill, *The Heart Don't Lie*, and her *Greatest Hits, Volume II* album are just additional brilliant jewels in her crown.

More than anything, Reba is a pioneer in stretching the traditional Nashville sound into the wide-ranging parameters that today's country music now encompasses. Not content to pigeonhole herself with one musical style, in 1988 she covered the soulful Aretha Franklin hit "Respect" on her *Reba* album, and suddenly she was expanding her vocal talents into such diverse directions as rock, soul, and blues, while remaining firmly within a country realm.

Since that time she has extended the boundaries and pushed the envelope of country music by tackling such controversial topics as euthanasia ("Bobby"), parental abandonment ("The Greatest Man I Never Knew"), and the problems of the elderly in America ("All Dressed up and Nowhere to Go").

There is a song on her *It's Your Call* album called "For Herself," in which Reba sings about a headstrong girl determined to take the reins of her own life and make her own mistakes. Reba wrote the song with two other women, but admits that the heroine in the song is suspiciously similar to herself. "It was pretty much me," she concedes, "I'm the type of person who's very bullheaded."

An exciting song stylist, Reba craves dramatic ballads, and enlivens them with conviction and electrifying panache. Songs like Bobbie Gentry's "Fancy," Vicki Lawrence's "The Night the Lights Went out in Georgia" and her own "Is There Life Out There" have presented her with the platform to launch her own budding acting career. The "minimovie" videos that accompanied those three songs have enticed Hollywood casting directors to pursue Reba for a variety of projects.

Taking her cue from Dolly Parton, Reba has the talent and drive to have an acting career that stands on its own merit. Having made her film debut in the 1990 sci-fi cult film *Tremors,* she landed the female lead in Kenny Rogers's 1991 four-hour TV mini-series "The Gambler IV." She is also at work on her own cinematic starring vehicle based on her hit song about a housewife going back to school to earn her diploma, "Is There Life Out There."

With twenty albums to her credit, Reba is the first solo contemporary female country artist to have a non-Greatest Hits studio album certified "Double Platinum" for over two million copies sold. She is also the only singer to ever be voted Female Vocalist of the Year four consecutive years by the Country Music Association. She has already racked up Grammies, American Music Awards, Academy

Of Country Music Awards, People's Choice Awards, and Country Music Association Awards, but what she really craves is an Academy Award for her acting.

"I want to win an Oscar," she proclaims. "It may take me a lot of years, but I do—I *want* to win an Oscar!"

Such aspirations may seem like a stretch coming from a country singer, but for Reba McEntire, lofty challenges and goals attained with determination and drive are what she is all about. In spite of her overwhelming fame and success, she is quite modest about her accomplishments. "I've never been to the top," she says humbly. "There is always somebody out there that's better, faster, wittier and does something different that sells more tickets or albums or is more popular. I've always been a bridesmaid." If that is the case, then she is obviously the bridesmaid who caught the bride's bouquet!

Self-motivated, with drive and grit, Reba McEntire is a talented and strong woman who has cut her own path to the top. Like the woman in the song "For Herself," Reba has never been one who was afraid to roll up her shirtsleeves and tackle whatever task or goal she currently has in her sights.

She was born March 28, 1955 in McAlester, Oklahoma. Reba's father, Clark, was a rancher who roped on the local rodeo circuit, and her mother, Jacqueline, was a schoolteacher. They were both influential in her life. She learned to love the ranch and rodeo life from her father, and her mother instilled in her the confidence to pursue a career and to go after her own dreams.

"My father, Clark McEntire, was a world-champion steer roper," explains Reba. "He and Mama invested his rodeo winnings in an 8,000-acre ranch near Chockie, a small town in southeastern Oklahoma. That's where I learned to ride and sing. Mama was blessed with a beautiful voice many have compared with Patsy Cline's. She wanted to pursue a singing career, but instead, she taught us kids how to sing three-part harmony to pass the time while we were on the rodeo circuit with Daddy."

In 1960, the Cheyenne Frontier Days Rodeo was the site of the auspicious PAID singing debut of Reba McEntire. She was five years old at the time, and she talked her brother Pake into accompanying her on a duet version of "Jesus Loves Me," in front of a bunch of cowboys. After Reba and Pake were finished, one of the cowboys gave Reba a nickel for the performance. "Even though I earned it — I was amazed," recalls Reba. "After that I was hooked!"

Growing up on a ranch, and around the rodeo world, both Reba and Pake became proficient at horseback riding. As a teenager, Reba competed in horseback barrel races. Simultaneously, she continued to explore her singing talents as well. Originally, she was most greatly influenced by Dolly Parton's and Loretta Lynn's singing styles. It was her mother who persuaded Reba to quit mimicking Dolly and Loretta, and concentrate on sounding like Reba. Obviously, the advice paid off!

In 1974, at Oklahoma City's prestigious National Finals Rodeo, Reba was asked to sing "The Star Spangled Banner" at the start of the festivities. As fate would have it, in the audience that day was rodeo-riding country-singer Red Steagall. When Steagall heard Reba's belting version of the national anthem, he asked to meet her. They chatted about the music business, and Red came away from their talk impressed by Reba's poise and on-stage confidence.

By this time, Reba was a student at Southeastern Oklahoma State University. Music was her major focus, and she studied piano and the classical violin. What she remembers most about her brief college career was that she "analyzed Mozart every which way."

According to Reba, "About a month later, I was back in school at Southeastern Oklahoma State in Durant, Oklahoma, when Mama got a call from Red. He said, 'Do you think you could get Reba down here to cut a demonstration tape?' Pake had already decided he would rather rodeo than sing, and [little sister] Susie wasn't even out of high school. I became the first McEntire guinea pig to enter the entertainment world."

Reba was signed to Mercury Records in 1976. She was so excited to be cutting her first album that she nearly blew out the sound equipment on the very first song. "It was a real pretty ballad, and when I got to the powerful part, I stayed right on the microphone—and the [sound meter] needles just disappeared!" How did they complete the recording amid her belting? "They asked me to back up!" laughs Reba.

Also, that very same year Reba married one of the professional cowboys that she had met on the rodeo circuit in Oklahoma, Charlie Battles. From 1976, until her divorce from Battles in 1988, Reba divided her time between recording, the concert trail, and rodeos with Charlie. Their home during those years was a cattle ranch that they owned in her home state.

In 1978 she released her first album, *Reba McEntire,* and began racking up country hits like "(You Lift Me) Up to Heaven" and "There Ain't No Future in This." She consistently released albums, including *Out Of A Dream* (1979), *Feel The Fire* (1980), *Heart To Heart* (1981), *Unlimited* (1982), *Behind The Scenes* (1983), *Just a Little Love* (1984), *My Kind of Country* (1984), and *Have I Got a Deal for You* (1985).

Along the way, Reba did make several changes until she discovered the right formula for success that would work for her. She changed record labels in 1984 with her "Just a Little Love" marking her debut in her present home—MCA Records. With the 1985 *Have I Got a Deal for You* album, Reba stopped relying on the judgment of outside producers to define her sound. From that album forward, Reba has co-produced every successive release with Jimmy Bowen. In that way she has control over every song.

According to Reba, "As my co-producer, Jimmy Bowen, said to me when I started producing my own records, 'No one knows better than you what's right for Reba McEntire.' "

Although she was coasting along with a nice little career—circa 1985, none of her albums sold more than a couple of hundred thousand copies each. With the exception of Dolly Parton, female artists weren't really building million-selling careers in country music, and Reba felt that it was time to change things.

McEntire explains, "The women in the audience are the ones who buy the music. So [former manager] Bill Carter told me one day, 'You know, you keep saying that you want to beat out all the groups and outsell the men in country music.' He said, 'You're gonna have to figure out why they sell more than you.' So we came to a conclusion that that was why: women buy the tickets and women buy the music. So, I started listening to songs that would appeal to women. *Whoever's In New England,* that was the album we tried that on—and it was my first 'Gold' album."

The strategy worked brilliantly. Not only did Reba net a Grammy Award for 1986 hit *Whoever's In New England,* but it also became her first video performance. The Academy Of Country Music and *Music City News* proclaimed the video version of *New England* the Top Country Video of 1987. Suddenly Reba's appeal began to blossom and grow.

When she released her fourteenth album, *The Last One to Know,* even *Rolling Stone* magazine chose to write about it. The review glowed that Reba was "a master of country classicism" who is excelling by bringing country music into the late 1980s marketplace by combining traditional country music with contemporary themes including a woman stuck in abusive marriage ("The Stairs"), and a Mexican man's idealistic view of the United States ("Just across the Rio Grande").

With reference to "The Stairs," Reba's singing delivery is so heartfelt because of her own personal passion for the topic. "Just because someone's bigger than you, it doesn't give him the right to hit you. Women need to know that!"

Just as she had taken stronger control of her song selection, she also noted that the new themes she was tackling directly interpreted into more concert ticket sales. Reba remembers that: "[It] was a goal for a long time to sell 5,000 [concert] tickets and now we're getting 10,000 consistently. When we package real good, we advertise real well, the shows have been selling out the first day."

In 1987 it was time for more changes in Reba's life. This time around, she took control of her personal life. Her marriage to Charlie had crumbled, and it was finally time to leave Oklahoma for Nashville. She was truly reaching for the brass ring this time around.

According to her, reading the Bible gave her the inner resolve to follow her instincts. "The Scripture

I was reading at that time really gave me a lot of strength," she distinctly remembers. "It said, 'The person who is behind the mule plow in the field and looks back is a fool.' So whatever I do from here on, 'Look ahead, and don't look back.' At the same time I was going through the divorce, I did nothing but plow on. I worked, I changed my life, moving from Oklahoma to Tennessee, just staying busy and trying to think up bigger and better things to do in my career."

One of the most exciting parts of Reba's career expansion was her transition into acting. When she was considered for a role in the production of the film *Tremors,* Reba jumped at the opportunity. "I *chose* to get into acting just to see what it was like to try it, to see if I could do it; to see if I would be accepted in the movie industry," says Reba, who concedes, "I cheated because I went on my name; you can always get in a bit easier if you have a name already." Well, she soon found that the name Reba McEntire definitely got her in the casting director's door.

Although it was "Reba McEntire, singing star" who landed the role, Ms. McEntire set out to prove that she was worthy of having been hired for the job. According to her, "Once I got the part, then I thought, 'I wonder how many aspiring young actresses read for this part, dying to get it, and it's like my summer vacation.' I took it more seriously then. I really started working hard because I don't want to take anything away from anybody who deserves it more than I do. And then it became a big deal for me for it to work, for me to do good."

Reba recalls, "*Tremors* was my first movie. I read for the part two or three times—they weren't convinced that Reba McEntire, who lives a glamorous life on the road, could be out in the desert with no makeup and her hair pulled back for two months. It was a big challenge for me—I wanted to prove myself to Hollywood. I said, 'Give me the dirt part. I'll take it, I'll do my best.' The only time I complained, is when they didn't have a Port-A-Potty down there on location. I was in the desert, drinking water like a camel, and I had to go to the bathroom. Well, the guys, of course, are going behind the little shrubs. There were snakes everywhere, and I was not going to get bit on the butt by a rattlesnake! I called my agent and said, 'I don't want to complain, but all I want is a Port-A-Potty out here.' "

Tremors is really a very tongue-in-cheek, campy, science-fiction film. Reminiscent of 1950s monster-from-outer-space flicks, it is about a herd of ground-burrowing man-eating worms threatening a community of desert dwellers. It stars Kevin Bacon as Valentine McKee and Fred Ward as Earl Bass, the two men who discover the creatures. The character that Reba plays is that of a modern rural housewife, Heather Gummer. Her husband in the film, Burt Gummer, is played by Michael Gross of TV's "Family Ties." Both Reba and Michael portray characters who are gung-ho gun-toting survivalists.

Reba is absolutely hysterical, wielding an Uzi machine gun, and passionately filling these ferocious earthworms from Mars full of lead. Feisty, strong, and not about to let these gigantic worms ruin the neatly organized basement recreation room of her house, Reba vividly brings to life a lively character, not too far off base from her own personality. With *Tremors* successfully under her belt, she began to actively look forward to roles in front of the cameras.

Having relocated herself and her band to Nashville, Tennessee, Reba was on the launching pad for an even bigger career success. With cross-over appeal on her mind, she strongly stated at the time, "I'm just as good and just as capable as anybody else [in show business], male or female. I don't think there's anything I can't do." With that, she set out to prove her point.

Little did she know at the time, but one of the men who was going to help her the most was right under her nose. Narvel Blackstock had joined her band in 1980 as a steel guitar player. Slowly, they had fallen in love, and in 1989 were married. By this point, Narvel also became Reba's manager. Together they moved into a four-story antebellum mansion forty-five miles out of Nashville. On February 12, 1990 Reba gave birth to her first child, Shelby Steven McEntire Blackstock, and like her mother before her — Reba entered the ranks of modern working mothers.

During her final months of pregnancy, Reba did

something really rare—she took some time off. "I was off five months when Shelby was born, and I could really tell the difference in my album sales. We were getting *returns*." It wasn't long before she was back at work.

There was never any question that Reba would immediately return her focus to her career. According to her, "Mama worked all the time. She said, 'The most important thing is you spend time with your children, then you go do your own thing and let the child play by himself. Don't feel like you have to give work time and play time to the child; you have to have time to yourself, and the child has to have time to himself.' "

While she made all of these changes in her personal life, her career jumped into full swing. Having relocated to Nashville, Reba had also changed co-producers to work with Tony Brown. In 1990 Reba released her big breakthrough album, *Rumor Has It*. From that album on, Reba began only choosing songs that show off women in roles who are in control of their own destiny—strong women who aren't afraid to grab the steering wheel of their fate in life.

"I think women need to be strong!" exclaims Reba. "My mother is one of the strongest people I've ever met in my life. She can cry right along with you at the saddest movie, but when the tension is there, she's the backbone. I do think I've made a conscious effort to record more songs for women. It's about time someone focused on them. I think

women are special, and I want to make them realize
that."

Although her 1987 *Greatest Hits* album had consistently sold, and became Reba's first "Platinum"
certified million-seller, *Rumor Has It* became her
first new studio album to almost instantly sell a
million copies. Over the past decade Reba had
grown and evolved to become the embodiment of
the nineties woman. The first cut on the album,
"Climb That Mountain High" isn't just a rousing
up-tempo song—it's an anthem, a proclamation of
self-worth and personal fulfillment. "Rumor Has
It" is a song about a woman confronting her cheating man. On "That's All She Wrote," Reba plays the
part of a woman who knows about the other
woman and is willing to take her man back—but
only if he pulls his act together. With the smashing
remake of Bobbie Gentry's "Fancy," Reba takes the
dramatic stance of a woman forced to become a
call girl as a means to escape her dirt-poor beginnings. The way Reba sings the song, and performs
it in the video, she relates the story of the "white
trash" girl named Fancy—in a fashion that doesn't
even hint at guilt or shame. She is a woman
who did what she had to do to survive. The entire *Rumor Has It* album reflects the es-
sence of Reba herself—a strong woman in total
control.

One of the most immediately striking aspects of
the *Rumor Has It* album is the cover photo itself.
"I like to shock people," explains Reba. "I like to

come up with new and different things. On the *Rumor Has It* cover, for instance, we had a photo of me with my hair under a hat. MCA Records said, 'Your hair is your trademark.' No, my trademark is my *voice*. I'm not going to strip stark naked and set my hair on fire, but I do like doing bitty things to keep life interesting."

When the album was released, it was destined to become her biggest hit album to date. Unfortunately, just as she was beginning to enjoy her greatest success, tragedy struck. At the time, Reba's touring entourage included bandleader and keyboard player Kirk Capello, bassist Terry Jackson, drummer Tony Saputo, guitarist and back-up singer Chris Austin, guitarist Michael Thomas, keyboard player Joey Cigainero, background singer Paula Kaye Evans, saxophone player Joe McGlohon, steel guitar player Pete Finney, road manager Jim Hammon, and her manager/husband Narvel Blackstock. Hammon had been with Reba for years, having worked his way up within her organization to become her road and tour manager. On Saturday, March 15, 1991, Reba was booked for a concert date at a private corporate convention for IBM employees. The 75-minute show that Reba performed that night was at the Sheraton Harbor Island Hotel. Reba and her band were due in Fort Wayne, Indiana for a concert the next night. It was just another weekend in the life of a jet-setting singing star.

That night Reba had complained of being

plagued by a bout of bronchitis. Narvel convinced
Reba to stay in San Diego to get some rest, and
they would fly to Ft. Wayne the following day.
Band members Capello, Jackson, Saputo, Austin,
Thomas, Cigainero, Evans, and road manager
Hammon all boarded a private jet at Brown Field,
just south of San Diego. The plane took off at 1:40
A.M. Saturday morning. Within minutes the twin-
engine Hawker Siddeley jet they were riding in
clipped a protruding rock near Otay Mountain. The
plane spun around like a pinwheel and crashed into
the mountain. All of the passengers aboard were
instantly killed.

Recalls Reba, "When I first heard something had
happened, it was 2:30 in the morning, and Narvel
and I were in a sound sleep at our hotel in San
Diego. Then the phone rings and our pilot says,
'Narvel, please come to my room.' And of course
Narvel just started jerking on his clothes and his
shoes. All he said was 'I think there's been an accident. Just go to sleep and I'll be back.' Of course I
couldn't go back to sleep." What she had awakened
to was her worst nightmare.

On Saturday night Reba and Narvel flew back to
Nashville. They first stopped at their home to see
Shelby, and then to visit Jim Hammon's wife
Debbie and their two sons. At the time she remem-
bers feeling absolutely numb with grief, and she
didn't know what to do about her career.

"We were wondering what to do," she recalls. "I
was wanting to cancel everything until July. I said,

'I'm just not going to go back out there. It's too much, I can't do it without them.' I told Debbie I had to make a decision. And she looked at me, just like Jim would have done and said, 'Are you thinking about quitting?' I said, 'Well, no, but I don't know when I can go back.' And she said, 'Jim Hammon worked all this time to help get you where you are today. He'd kick your butt if you thought about quitting.' And I hugged her neck and said, 'I needed that, you're right.' I know Jim would tell me, 'Now Reba, you know those fans expect that out of you, and you can't quit; you've worked too hard and too long, and you've got to get back up there.' "

Suddenly Reba knew what she had to do. According to her, "I had two band members who survived, and I knew that if I didn't get them back on stage right away, they'd be just like me—they probably *couldn't* get back on stage again. I know that the band members who died would prefer that I go on. That's what we did, after all, for a living. Eight people got killed. But if they stepped right back in this room, I know they'd say, 'Reba, we're proud of you for going on.' "

Reba was deluged with millions of letters of condolence from her fans. She recalls, "I signed thank-you notes for three weeks."

Several of Reba's friends in the business— including Dolly Parton—called her up and offered her the use of their musicians. According to her, "Dolly called me and said, 'You need my band?

You take them.' The Oak Ridge Boys said the same thing. That's the way everybody was — 'We'll do anything in the world.' "

One of the people who called Reba up was country legend Waylon Jennings. Over thirty years earlier, Jennings had been Buddy Holly's bass player. On February 3, 1959, Waylon gave up his seat on a private plane to make room for J. P. Richardson (a/k/a The Big Bopper) — the singer of "Chantilly Lace." Also on the plane were Buddy Holly, and Richie Valens — hot from his first hit, "La Bamba." The plane crashed right after take-off.

In his conversation with Reba, Waylon said to her, "Don't let guilt set in, don't let guilt even touch you." She knew that she had to pick up the pieces immediately and go back to work. She was booked to sing the song "I'm Checking Out" from the film *Postcards from the Edge* on the upcoming Academy Awards broadcast only days later. She decided to use that as her return to performing. Reba said before the show, "I'm going to do it for the band. They're checking out. They've got a new place to dwell."

Ironically, one of the last songs that Reba performed that last tragic night with her band, was Patsy Cline's mournfully blue "Sweet Dreams." Cline had been killed in a similar plane crash in 1963. "That might be the last time I sing it," Reba pondered only days after the accident.

Over a year later, Reba was still analyzing the situation, and the impact that it had on her life.

"Everything changed," she reflected. "I married a man I totally love, love to be with, respect, admire, trust. I had Shelby with him. With Shelby it was total happiness and bliss; he gave me something in my life that I had never been given before. When the tragedy happened, I felt like saying, 'Screw this. I don't ever want to love anybody else again; I don't ever want to get close to anybody.' On the other hand, that's not the lesson to learn from this. It's love every minute you can, live life to the fullest each minute as if it is your last. Learn from it — get your ducks in a row, get right with God. 'Where do you go?' 'What do you believe in?' 'What do you feel in your heart is the right thing to do?' I grew immensely. I went within myself; I was a pretty outward person, and I'm more of an inward person now. I listen more; I'm quieter. I was never mad at God. I knew that it happened for a reason, so I trusted Him; I know He knows best."

Throughout the months following the accident, Reba took a cold, hard look at reality. "It made me realize that my time can be any minute, Narvel's time can be any minute, so could Shelby's, my mom, dad, brother and sisters," said Reba. "I don't think I'll ever get over it. I don't think anybody gets over something like that." With thoughts like that running through her head, Reba dove into her work with a vengeance.

Two separate projects put McEntire back onto the road of the living. When she was offered a role in Kenny Rogers's 1991 two-part four-hour TV movie,

"The Luck of the Draw: The Gambler Returns," the fourth installment of his popular "Gambler" movies — she grabbed it. For Reba, the opportunity represented a six-week shooting schedule that would give her a rest from touring, and time to concentrate on something other than the trauma of her grief.

In the plot of "The Luck Of The Draw:, The Gambler Returns," Reba portrayed the role of Burgundy Jones, a flamboyant ex-madam bankrolling a red-hot poker game in San Francisco. One of the most exciting aspects of the movie, was the chance for Reba to work with several TV Western heroes recreating their famous roles, including Gene Berry as Bat Masterson, Clint Walker as "Cheyenne" Bodie, Chuck Connors as The Rifleman — Lucas McCain, and Hugh O'Brien as Wyatt Earp. Also in the film was screen legend Mickey Rooney as a pioneer filmmaker. The experience was a growing one for her career, and a healing one for her heart.

Amid production, Reba excitedly beamed, "I have quite a few good scenes in this movie. I get to shoot a Gatling gun. In another, I knock a guy out. I get to tell off Kenny's character, Brady Hawkes. I get shot. People try to steal my money. It's an exciting part and lot of fun to do." The end result was quite successful, and Reba ended up with the majority of favorable reviews for her acting, and colorful portrayal of equally feisty Burgundy Jones.

According to her, "The best thing about this character is that she's a lot like me, and I can put a lot of my own character into her. Maybe that's because I don't know anything about acting!"

When *USA Today* reviewed "The Luck of the Draw: The Gambler Returns," the only thing that they liked in the whole film was Reba. The newspaper especially delighted at "the rib-tickling sight of Reba McEntire as an ex-madam in hip-hugging black leather."

Reba's other project on the road to recovery was recording her next album, the fittingly entitled *For My Broken Heart*. When it came time to select material for the album, Reba insisted that the album was going to reflect her mood. In other words she was going straight for the heart on each and every cut. She explained, "I think misery loves company; that's the songs I wanted to sing. I had a lot of good, uptempo, happy songs pitched to me—I didn't even want to hear them. I didn't want to say anything that was short of ripping your heart out."

She further explained, "It wasn't even a concern whether it sold. My producer Tony Brown said, 'You've got to have an uptempo song on there. You just can't put out an album without an uptempo song.' I said, 'I don't want to hear anything "up," and I don't want to sing it.' "

Well, she was in a blue mood, and she conveyed each song with such heartbreak and painful conviction, that it has been acknowledged as one of the finest albums of her career. The title track set the tone for the brilliant set of ten songs. The subject matter includes a neglected old woman in a nursing home ("All Dressed Up [With Nowhere to Go]"), the regrets of lost love ("I Wouldn't Go That Far"), a husband who is put in jail for killing his terminally ill wife ("Bobby"), a murder of passion ("The Night the Lights Went Out in Georgia"), and the mournful goodbye to a lost loved one ("If I Had Only Known"). It was a tour de force of drama and pain, and it became her fastest-selling album ever.

"It's a very touchy situation," Reba analyzed, "I've always been a big believer that my best songs are ballads." Evidently, she knows what she's talking about!

Two of Reba's most stunning videos were culled from the *For My Broken Heart* album. The murder-mystery melodrama of "The Night the Lights Went Out in Georgia" was a perfect vehicle to turn into a "mini-drama," complete with Reba in makeup as an old lady recounting the events of that fateful Georgia night. In the video for "Is There Life Out There," Reba is seen as a housewife returning to school while still running the household. Rock star Huey Lewis starred as Reba's husband in the video. It is a serious goal of Reba's to expand this video into a TV movie in much the same way that Kenny Rogers did with the song "The Gambler."

One of the things that Reba is the most proud of is the impact that video had on women across the country. According to her, " 'Is There Life Out There' has sent many, many women back to school. I get at least two women a night saying, 'I'm graduating from high school,' or 'I'm going to get my

GED,' or 'I'm going back to college.' It's really, really neat."

In the liner notes of this album, Reba wrote a message proclaiming that the songs reflected her state of mind at the time, and hopefully it would aid in the healing of several broken hearts in the world. Apparently it worked like magic.

When she was finished with her role in the *Gambler* film, and the recording of her album, Reba hit the concert trail, and picked up where she left off before the tragedy. Before the year was up she also taped a Bob Hope Christmas special for NBC-TV, and her own two-part holiday special called "Reba McEntire's Christmas Card" on TNN.

In July of 1992, Reba dropped in on her favorite afternoon TV soap opera, "One Life to Live." How this came about was the fact that one of the show's regular cast members, Susan Battan, who plays the character Luna Moody, is a huge Reba fan. It was Battan who made it her personal mission to get McEntire onto the show.

Battan explained of her successful quest, "I was going down to the Azalea Festival in North Carolina and I knew she was going to be singing there. My plane got in too late and I missed the concert. I called and had them tell her I was coming and that I wanted to meet her. So, a sheriff met me at the airport to take me over, so that I wouldn't miss her. She was waiting backstage and I went in and I talked to her. I said, 'The producers have said that I can come and officially beg you to please be on the

show.' Reba said, 'Absolutely. I'd love to!' I thought
it was going to be really hard, but she really
watches all the ABC soaps and follows them. She
wanted to come and do it."

In the plot of the soap, Reba played herself in
two different episodes of the show, as a high-school
friend of Luna's. Reba and her new band performed two songs, "Is There Life Out There" and
"The Greatest Man I Never Knew," and she had
some light dialogue with Battan's character of
Luna. "I really wanted to play one of the bad
guys," claimed Reba. "I would love to come back as
Reba's evil twin sister, the black sheep of the family!"

When it came time to go back into the studio to
record the follow-up to "For My Broken Heart,"
Reba decided that she still had a wealth of sad
songs to sing, and christened 1992 *It's Your Call*
album "For My Broken Heart, Chapter Two." In
the liner notes, Reba penned, "I hope all our hearts
have healed a little and continue to grow in life and
love."

Again high on the drama, the subject matter of
the songs on Reba's twentieth album runs the gamut
of emotions. On "It's Your Call" Reba finds herself
fielding a phone call from the other woman, getting
jilted on "He Wants to Get Married," blowing the
whistle on a cheating man on "Take It Back,"
yearning for an unobtainable love on "The Heart
Won't Lie," and resolving herself to loss on "Lighter
Shade Of Blue."

"It's Your Call" and the brilliant Vince Gill duet, "The Heart Won't Lie," are truly two of the best songs Reba has ever recorded. Both songs are delivered with such passion and fire, that it is easy to see why they both became huge top-ten hits for her.

Repeating the success of *For My Broken Heart,* the *It's Your Call* album also sold over two million copies, becoming her second "Double Platinum" smash LP in a row. Reviewing the album, *Time* magazine glowed, "Reba's pure country voice is a lariat across an abyss . . . On this album McEntire adds something special: a sort of time-to-put-myself-first feminism." *USA Today* proclaimed, "While it continues McEntire's particular strain of pain, the new album rebuilds her image as a woman of sass and strength."

When Reba released her *Greatest Hits Volume II* album in October of 1993, it debuted in the Top Ten, and by Christmas it was also "Double Platinum." The album's trajectory was aided by the hot new hit single she released off of it only weeks before, "Does He Love You," a smash Top Ten duet with Reba's new discovery—Linda Davis. The "wife vs. mistress" theme of the song was enhanced by a humorously sparkling "cat fight" video with Rob Reiner as director. In the last moments of the "Does He Love You" video, jealous Reba is seen detonating a bomb planted in the power boat Davis and the man-in-question are aboard.

On the *Country Music Association Awards* telecast that September, Reba stirred up quite a controversy when she and Linda performed the song. During the number, voluptuous Reba was wearing a flame red dress with an eye-popping plunging neckline and a see-through mesh décolletage. She looked fabulous in it, and that number became one of the most talked-about aspects of the program. Reba *is* country music's reigning diva, and she made sure she stole the show in that dress! Mission accomplished.

In the country-music world, and in the greater show-business scheme of things, Reba McEntire has it all. Not only is she country music's first "Double Platinum"-selling female, she is the girl most likely to succeed in establishing a full-fledged acting career. She admits, "Live shows are really my love, but I'll take another movie if the script is right and the director."

With her career swimmingly exciting, focused, and ultra-successful, Reba McEntire is truly in the superstar category in 1990s country music. However, she hasn't "gone Hollywood" with her personal life. Today, she and Narvel and Shelby live on an eighty-acre lot, in their huge yellow-brick mansion. Says Reba, "We've got a pool and a pool house and a tennis court and a five-stall horse barn." Although she lives the "country life," make no mistake about it — it is the *glamorous* country life! Making a joke about the pronunciation of the word spelled r-o-d-e-o, Reba laughs, "If you're riding in it, it's *road*-ee-oh. In Los Angeles, when you go shopping, it's Row-*day*-oh Drive!"

In today's country-music scene, it is clear that Reba McEntire is a talented overachiever. According to her, "No matter what you achieve in life, you're always wondering, 'Is there something I should be doing? Is there something I'm missing?' " In the case of Reba McEntire there isn't a single thing missing—in fact she has it all! The million-selling records, the awards, the wonderful family life, the budding acting career, and her inner and outer beauty make it clear that she is one star who is here to stay. In the music industry, which is full of flash-in-the-pan performers, Reba McEntire is truly a glamorous original whose reign at the top has just begun!

Chapter Two
Wynonna

Of all of the women in country music today, Wynonna Judd has had the longest time on the solo career launching pad. With nine years as one half of the mother and daughter singing duo, The Judds, Wynonna has had nearly a decade as a country star to mentally, vocally, and emotionally prepare herself to become the solo singing star she is today.

She is also country music's most reluctant solo star as well. If her mother, Naomi Judd, hadn't contracted chronic active hepatitis and been forced to retire, this chapter title would have been "The Judds" instead of "Wynonna." However, in the two years since her first solo flight, she has exceeded all expectations, and is one of today's two "Double Platinum"-selling country gals (Reba is the other one); and Wynonna's solo debut album in 1992 made her contemporary country music's first "Triple Platinum" female artist.

Her first two solo albums, *Wynonna* and *Tell Me Why* were almost instant million sellers, and her solo concert performances have been sold-out successes since the minute she began to fly alone. She is such a huge star that her albums disappear off the store shelves based on her name alone. *Wynonna* sold a million copies the first week it was released, and *Tell Me Why* took only a fortnight to perform the same feat.

The promise in her voice, the gutsy way she can phrase a lyric, and the emotion that she can express with a song have made her one of the hottest singers on the music charts—male or female—country or rock. Having shortened her performing moniker to the one word Wynonna, puts her in the Cher and Madonna league of one-name superstar clout.

It wasn't so long ago that her solo fate was uncertain. When Wynonna and Naomi disbanded The Judds in 1991, it was unclear which way the chips were going to fall. Anyone who had attended a Judds concert in the past knew the score. Gregarious and glamorous Naomi had all of the on-stage personality in the family. She sashayed and danced about the stage amid the show, chatted with the audience, flirted with the band, and effortlessly charmed everyone in sight. Wynonna was the one who stayed stationary, strummed her guitar, and only tentatively made eye contact with her audience. However, it was Wynonna who had the full-throttle voice. She sang with power and passion, while Naomi sang the strongly supportive harmony vocals that defined The Judds' unique sound.

Family members make the best harmony singers.
Listen to any old Andrews Sisters record, or one
by the Jackson Five, the Pointer Sisters, or
Brother Phelps. Singing siblings especially—
usually have similar vocal timbres and ranges.
When the Judds burst onto the scene in 1983,
they not only looked like sisters, but they sounded
like sisters as well. They had the same vocal
scope, and identical phrasing. On television and in
their first videos it was almost impossible to tell
which one was the mother and which one was the
daughter. It was like one of those dishwashing
soap commercials where the viewer was asked to
view and compare a mother's and daughter's
hands.

The duo proceeded to rack up every imaginable
musical award. In 1984, 1985, 1986, 1988, and
1991 The Judds won Grammy Awards in the category of Best Country Performance By A Duo Or
Group With Vocal. In addition Naomi (along with
Paul Overstreet and John Jarvis) won a Best
Country Song Grammy Award for the composition "Love Can Build a Bridge."

When The Judds called it quits because of
Naomi's health—all eyes were on Wynonna. "Can
she cut it alone?" everyone asked. "Does she have
the confidence to go from being 'the shy one' in
a world-famous duo, to solo stardom?" It was
so perfectly clear to their fans that Wynonna
was completely happy to let Mom be the coquet-
tish vamp on stage, while she herself was "the

voice" of the operation.

Well, hallelujah—the caterpillar has emerged from her spotlight-shy cocoon—and she is a genuine solo hit-making butterfly on her own! And, the additional good news is the fact that on Wynonna's albums, Naomi is nicely represented on several songs on which she either sings harmony vocals, or contributes compositions.

According to Wynonna, including Mom on her albums seemed like a logical transitional move. "It just seemed so natural," she claims. "I know that Mom was saying to me the other day, 'You know, you and I are going to be in each other's lives for a long, long time.' And, it's so natural for me to go back to what gave birth to me. I mean, it's just as natural as breathing for me to get her involved with my music. She's taught me pretty much everything I know as far as how to follow my good instincts, how to believe in myself when everything else around me is turmoil and chaos."

Although she was once a reluctant stage performer, with one hearing of Wynonna's albums you know that she is living the role she was born to play. When she is singing Mary-Chapin Carpenter's autobiographical composition about relating better to her guitar than to the opposite sex, "Girls with Guitars," you know that the lyrics strike a familiar chord with Wynonna as well.

Wynonna admits that as a child, the only thing she cared about was playing her guitar. "I was very lazy, just lying in my room playing my guitar and singing. Mom worried about me. She'd try to cow-prod me to get out and do things, and I rebelled against that. It was frustrating for her to work double shifts, come home and see me doing nothing but music." That all seems to be a lifetime ago.

Wynonna was born Christina Claire Ciminella, May 30, 1964, in Ashland, Kentucky. Her mother, Naomi, who was born Diana Ellen Judd, had married her high school sweetheart, Michael Ciminella when she was seventeen. The week of her high school graduation, and four months after the wedding, she gave birth to Christina. The family moved to California, and following the birth of a second daughter, Ashley, and eight years of marriage, Diana and Michael divorced.

To support herself and her two daughters, Diana worked as a model, and as a secretary. In 1976 she returned to Kentucky, settling in Morrill, where she began nursing school. To entertain themselves and young Ashley, Diana and her daughter Christina would sit around the kitchen table singing, while Christina played the guitar. The duo quickly discovered how beautifully their voices blended together when they sang.

According to Christina/Wynonna, it was at the age of ten that she really began immersing herself in the world of music. "That was when I *discovered* music," she claims. "My influences—I thank God for this now—were records for the old record shops, the used bins. Bluegrass was my first influence, and the mountain harmonies, the mountain soul of Hazel And Alice, the harmonies of the family from The Delmore Brothers, The Stanley Brothers, and The Louvin Brothers. And then I started listening to Bonnie Raitt. She's been one of the biggest influences of my vocal style. Instead of Top 40, I was listening to big band, and I was listening to the stuff that my grandparents were going dancing to on the weekends. I was pretty eclectic."

When Christina was fifteen, Diana watched her oldest daughter crawling into an introverted shell. "It became my private world," she recalls. "I wanted to be in music more than anything in the whole world. Instead of worrying about me going out and drinking and driving, Mom was worried about me getting out of the house and getting a real job."

Working as a nurse at the time, Diana started recording some of her singing sessions with Christina, on a small tape recorder. When Diana medically treated the daughter of Nashville producer Brent Maher, the legacy of The Judds began to take wings.

Knocked out by the homemade tape that his daughter had presented him with, RCA Records' Nashville vice-president Joe Galante offered the mother/daughter team a recording deal. Dropping their complex last name, the duo took Diana's maiden name of Judd. Since they were going through an identity change, they decided that they needed glitzier first names, too. Mom Diana chose "Naomi" from the Bible, while Christina picked "Wynonna" from the song lyrics of "Route 66." (The song lyric refers to the actual town of Wynona, Oklahoma—with one less *n*)

In 1983 the newly rechristened pair released their first single, made it into the country Top 20, and their second single, the smooth ballad "Mama, He's Crazy," shot up to number one. The Judds' first album was really just a six song "EP," as RCA Records wasn't certain if the duo was going to find enough appeal to merit a whole album. Talk about tragic underestimation!

During their ten years as a recording duo, The Judds racked up one "Double Platinum" album, three "Platinum" albums, and six "Gold" albums. They placed an outrageous total of twenty-three hit singles on the country charts. In addition to that, they racked up enough music industry awards to fill an entire trophy room.

Everything seemed to be going swimmingly well for The Judds, having achieved international fame, and amassing a wealth of money and fans. Their sweet harmonies guided them consistently to the top of the record charts. However, on New Year's Day 1990, complaining of fatigue, Naomi made plans to visit her doctor. The following day, she was diagnosed as having chronic active hepatitis. Although it can be fatal, after months of tests and treatments, the ailment was put in temporary remission. However, it was imperative that Naomi bow out of the grueling life on the concert road. In late 1990 it was decided that The Judds would do one year-and-a-half-long "farewell" tour, leaving ample rest time for Naomi between concert dates. The beginnings of planning a solo career for Wynonna were put into gear while the last Judds tour progressed. On December 4, 1991, The Judds performed their last concert together, and it became a huge pay-per-view cable television megaevent. To fully commemorate the legacy of The Judds music, RCA released a 3-CD deluxe retrospect package called *The Judds Collection: 1983-1990*.

The following month, "live" on the air on "The American Music Awards" telecast, Wynonna debuted her soon-to-be-released first solo single "She Is His Only Need." It skyrocketed up the charts to number one. Voila! — a solo country singing legend was born. When her debut solo album, *Wynonna* was released on March 31, 1992, she was an instant hit. The album sold over three million copies, and spawned three number-one hit singles.

It was like being in a fishbowl for Wynonna. She knew that the expectations of her were lofty. The critics however gave her unanimous flying colors and hard-won accolades. "In one explosive thrust, it positions Wynonna among the top tier of country's most distinctive, compelling female entertainers," exclaimed *Country America* magazine. "Brash and confident . . . like a girl with the world at her fingertips," glowed *Mademoiselle*.

And, *Rolling Stone,* after awarding *Wynonna* four
stars pointed out her "powerful, stirring, enno-
bling music . . . 'Wynonna' has the feel of hard-
won personal revelation." Well, she was on her
way!

"When I started work on this album," Wynonna
explained at the time, "I really felt I was starting
all over again. My identity for the last [nine]
years—actually twenty-seven years—has been as
Naomi's kid. What if people aren't as interested in
Wynonna as they were in The Judds?" Boy, did
she ever underestimate her own self-worth!

At the time of the group's break-up, Wynonna
still lived in her mom's house. Sister Ashley had
since moved to Los Angeles to pursue an acting
career. Not only did the singing act, The Judds,
break up, but in 1992 Wynonna also physically
left home, and the protective arms of her mother.
With her solo career in the planning stages, it felt
odd to live under the same roof as her former
singing partner.

"At first, I would be in the house listening to
tapes and hear Mom drive in the driveway, and I'd
put them away. Part of me didn't want to go on
without her or have her see me going on without
her," Wynonna explains.

However, she was not entirely convinced that
she could cut the umbilical cord fully. To compro-
mise she began shopping for her own place—in
Mom's neighborhood. "I thought I'd buy land
next to hers," says Wynonna. "So we could be side

by side. And I wrestled with that decision because I thought, 'She's going to come over to my house every day. I won't be able to do anything without her knowing!' Because, I thought, 'You know what—that's okay, because she's my mother!' And, I know there are times when I'll need a free meal! Hey, why not just move in next door? So, I did buy land next to hers. I think it's interesting in this life that I'm leading, I realize now more than ever how important it is to have family in a day that's so transient—everybody is so freaked out and worried about everything. And, my mom says to me, 'Wynonna, we all need a place we can go that we can be ourselves.' "

Wynonna knew that the heat was on with her debut album. She realized that all eyes were on her, and she was scared stiff that it would be a disaster. "With the first album I felt devastated," she recalls. "I had to get up in the morning and go, 'Wynonna: I AM, I CAN, I WILL!' I had to talk to myself, have a lot of meetings with myself."

To take full circle the entire "trial by fire" bent that she was on, she immediately jumped on the solo concert trail. Although she was alone on stage, Mom was in the wings for the first week of the tour, adding moral support.

It wasn't long before loneliness set in. Amid the tour Wynonna proclaimed, "I go between one minute feeling like I can conquer the world, and the next minute wanting to call my mom and have her come get me. When I get to feeling sorry for myself or down from too much pressure, I stop and think how she must feel. When I'm up there singing and look over at her sitting at the monitor board looking up at me, I think how hard it must be for her to let go, not only as a mother, but as a professional partner. It's like a double whammy."

The pressures of the road are hard on all performers. Some of them drink too much. Some of them smoke too much. Some of them get involved in drugs. None of these obsessions ever interested Wynonna. However, there is a fourth on-the-road addiction to become obsessed with: food. Almost instantly, Wynonna began packing on the pounds. "I'm lonely and want to eat all the foods my mom gave me when I was a child. We all have our indulgences, and mine aren't alcohol or drugs, and I don't smoke. But *food* has been my reward, and frankly I've rewarded myself a lot," she admits.

In addition to breaking up with her singing partner, and technically leaving home, in the same fell swoop — Wynonna broke off her long-running engagement to singer Tony King of the Nashville singing group Matthews, Wright and King.

"We're still very friendly," Wynonna explains. "We're just not 'committed' to each other. I care a lot about him. I trust him, and I'm there for him if something happens and he needs me. But I need my time and my space right now to hear what God wants me to do. I have such a fear of marriage. In my mind, I have a fantasy picture of what marriage should be. And it's something I've never experienced. My mom and dad divorced when I was eight years old; let's just put it like that. So I'm really insecure in that area right now. I don't date. I don't have the luxury of being able to go out and meet somebody. Nor do I want to. When I discovered my independence, I started to enjoy being alone. I wanted to come home, draw my bath and be by myself. That's hard to tell someone who loves you because it makes them feel left out. I know Tony has felt left out, but I know I'm doing what I believe with all my heart God wants me to do. If God wants Tony and me to be together, we will be."

She instead occupies herself with a close circle of friends. According to her, "In my personal life I have friends that are diverse. I have friends that are responsible and have real jobs. I have real creative strange friends, and I have friends who are farmers and don't know anything about a Grammy Award. I try to do everything I can to represent those people and what they have to do with my life. I find myself in a lot of different situations in life, and maybe I'm speaking out about those situations through my music."

Due to her break-up with Tony King, and an on-stage slip of the tongue, rumors spread in 1992 that Wynonna was gay. As she explains it, "I remember one time I did a show out West, and I said, 'Welcome to my "coming out party." ' Where

I come from — that means a girl coming into womanhood. But a bunch of people wrote me letters. Everything I say is going to be turned around."

To blow off steam while on the concert trail, Wynonna takes off on solo rides on her Harley Davidson. The "motorcycle mama" image is part of her new more rock & roll image. "I wear a helmet," she proclaims. "Mom says it's okay as long as I don't start wearing tube tops and paint FOXY LADY on my motorcycle! The Harley gives me a chance to pull up beside fans just long enough for them to recognize me, and then I pull away. If you lose the child within yourself, you might as well give up."

Another of her tension-releasing bouts found her taking her debut bungee-cord jump. According to her, "One of the biggest fears I've ever had was going out on stage alone, which I conquered on April 2nd [1992]. And what do I do next? BUNGEE JUMPING! And, I'll never do it again, unless someone offers me a lot of money."

In 1993, when Wynonna released her second solo album, "Tell Me Why," it virtually rang with an exciting sense of self-confidence. Certified "Platinum" in fourteen days, it really galvanized Wynonna's solo identity and fame. Comparing the two albums, Wynonna explains, "First album — I never want to go through that again! Yet, I learned more about myself from that first album, and felt more alive, even though they say 'with every death comes life.' I kind of feel like I experienced the death of The Judds and then the rebirth of Wynonna. Yet now I realize there will always be The Judds. The Judds will always be, I hope, in people's memories and hearts. This first album was such a labor of love done during the first ten months of my life without Mom. And the second record—it's more like I've moved away from home. The first album had more of a connection with where I'd been. And now, thanks to fans encouraging me to be myself, I felt confident to do something even more different. It has some blues and just more of what I am as an artist. And that still includes my Appalachian influences of course."

To strike off into new territory, in 1993 Wynonna began formulating plans for a fantastic new concert tour with Clint Black, cleverly entitled "The Black and Wy Tour." To complete the connection, Wynonna recorded the Number One hit duet with Black entitled "A Bad Goodbye." According to Wynonna, Clint presented the song to her in a most bizarre fashion. "I was standing backstage at the CMA Anniversary Show [taping in January 1993], and Clint walked right up to me with his guitar, takes me into a broom closet and sings to me. Imagine that! Clint Black walks up to you, says, 'I want to sing you a song,' and takes you into a broom closet and sings you a song?!?"

Well, both the song and the tour were a smashing success, and just another feather in Wynonna's hit-making cap. Regarding the tour, Wynonna explained, "It just seemed like a good business decision to our managers. But, also, I like Clint Black a lot as a person. I remember when he first came out on the scene, there was something really unique about him. This was back before everybody was wearing a cowboy hat. We've worked together before. And in this business, one thing I'm learning more and more every day is, since life is so short, why not work with people you like? I just have been so blessed before to work with people that I love, like my mom—I had to throw that in there! And, I thought: 'This year I want to tour with somebody that *I like.*' And I like his music, and I think his music fits well with what I'm doing, and vice versa."

Looking at her life from a more relaxed perspective than her trial-by-terror year of 1991, Wynonna feels more confidently her own woman. "I'm a nineties kind of girl," she explains, "yet, I'm very old-fashioned in a lot of ways. I have very old-fashioned traditions and I was raised in a very Southern background. Yet, I want to go out to L.A. and shop and be cool and buy things and do things in the modern world, but sometimes I feel like I don't belong in this time. I feel like I was born in a time that was so chaotic that, I kind of think, 'Wow, what am I doing here?' Because I feel real differently sometimes than a lot of people do. All that comes out in my music."

According to her, her newfound independence is

addicting in itself. "I want to continue to bring into this music business creative freedom," she says. "I want to be able to go into that studio, spill my guts, and for no one to stand there and say, 'I'm sorry, you can't do that, because that is way out of line.'"

It is hard to imagine anyone saying no to Wynonna Judd in any terms (except for maybe her mother!) With a growing list of awards, and "Gold" and "Platinum" albums to her credit, I certainly hope that her new next-door-to-Naomi bachelorette pad has ample space for *her own* personal trophy room as well!

Chapter Three
Trisha Yearwood

At the age of twenty-nine, Trisha Yearwood is the epitome of a 1990s country singing star success story. "Something happens every day to make me feel like Cinderella," she beams enthusiastically. However, Cinderella's story seems drab by contrast. With her first two albums certified "Platinum" million-sellers, a high-profile Revlon cosmetics ad campaign, a growing list of music industry awards and an expanding movie and video career, in three short years Trisha has gone from "The Wrong Side of Memphis" to the right side of Nashville!

With her fresh-faced good looks and her expressively torchy vocals, Trisha Yearwood stands at the pinnacle of a full-fledged multi-media career gloriously in full bloom. Almost instantly—with her brilliant self-titled album—Trisha has gone from unanimously unknown to immediately unforgettable. She was such an immediate smash right out of the chute, that when it came time to record her second album, 1992's *Hearts in Armor,* she was joined with such guest-starring media contemporaries as Vince Gill, Emmylou Harris, and Glenn Frey. At one time she was a fan of theirs, and now they are fans of hers.

However, the first and foremost fan of all was none other than Garth Brooks himself. Garth and Trisha were friends in Nashville before Brooks became the number-one star of modern country music. They had a long-standing pact to help each other, regardless of who became famous first, and Garth kept his promise. It was Brooks's appearance on two songs on her first album that assured Yearwood immediate press and radio attention. Then when he asked her to be the opening act on his sold-out 1991 tour of America's biggest venues, Trisha skyrocketed to instant fame.

Of their meeting in 1989, Trisha recalls, "He was still not even on the radio yet, he hadn't even released his single yet. We became friends. He said he wanted to help out if he was ever able to." Well, he is obviously a man of his word!

The fireworks continued when Trisha released her third album, *The Song Remembers When*. The title cut zoomed up to the top of the charts, and Yearwood effortlessly perpetuated her reputation for consistent hit-making. On the LP Trisha saluted her idol, Ronstadt, by covering Linda's "Mr. Radio;" and by having former Ronstadt band member, Andrew Gold, singing harmony vocals with her on his composition "Better Your Heart Than Mine." Country veteran Willie Nelson is heard on the song "Hard Promises To Keep."

With such chart-topping hits as "She's in Love with the Boy," "The Song Remembers When" and "Down on My Knees," one of the keys to her phenomenal success is her ability to choose songs that show off her expressively gutsy and blues-tinged voice. Of her selection criteria, Trisha explains, "I think about the songs that really tear me apart, and there are songs that I hear and I go, 'Wow, how'd they know that about me?!' or 'that really makes me feel what they're saying, and makes me believe what they're saying.' And, those are the kind of songs that I look for."

Born September 19, 1964 in Monticello, Georgia, Trisha Yearwood was the youngest of two daughters. Her father, bank vice-president Jack Yearwood, and mother, schoolteacher Gwen, encouraged Trisha and her older sister Beth, to become independent individuals. "My parents always encouraged us to do whatever we wanted to do," Trisha remembers. "When I told them I wanted to be a singer, they didn't think I was crazy. My sister and I always made good grades, and I think some people thought, 'What a shame. Trisha could have gone out and done something with her life.' Other people may have felt that way, but my parents never did."

Originally the family lived within the Monticello city limits, but eventually moved out to the country. Trisha regretted the move immensely. "I cried and cried," she recalls, "because we didn't have any neighbors out there. Now I can't wait until I can have thirty acres of my own. I don't want to live forever in a place where I don't even have a yard. I really miss having what I had then — going to sleep at night and having it be totally dark and quiet, not hearing any sirens. You could even lay out naked in the backyard — unless you heard the postman coming up the drive!"

Trisha was a tomboy as a young girl. Her mother remembers, "It seems like she was always getting X-rays and stitches. She was constantly running around outside." She once ran out of the house so preoccupied with the baseball glove on her hand that she failed to see the four-by-four wooden beam protruding from the back of her father's truck. That little error in judgment represented four of her dozens of stitches.

A natural-born entertainer, Patricia, as she was known back then caught the "bug" at an early age. "When I was growing up, I wanted to do every kind of performing. I did talent shows and plays and musicals and just anything I could do to perform."

Of her teenage years, Trisha confides, "My best friend was Melinda Sauls. She was a year older than me, and that was cool, because she could drive. She was also a lifeguard down at the pool — a glamorous job. In the summer, we'd hang out at the pool, get fabulous tans and scope on guys who never wanted anything to do with us. Melinda let me drive her car one time when I wasn't old enough to drive. Her mom saw us, and we got

in trouble. Other than that, we were pretty harm-
less."

When she was growing up, Trisha's musical idol
was Linda Ronstadt—starting with Ronstadt's
"Heart Like a Wheel" album. "I probably have
every record she ever made," she claims. "I think
she could sing the phone book and make it sound
beautiful."

She further explains, "I always listened to a lot
of different music. I might be in the mood for
Linda one day, then for Hank Williams or Patsy
Cline the next day, and Elvis the next day. What I
do now is probably a combination of all those."

After high school she shortened her given name
of "Patricia" down to "Trisha," and enrolled for
two years at a local junior college. From there she
transferred to Nashville's Belmont College, where
she studied business, with a particular focus on
the music business. Through an internship program, she began working at Mary Tyler Moore's
short-lived record label, MTM Records. She
started out in the publicity department, and
learned very quickly the value of publicity in a
well-planned show-business career. She also began
supplementing her income by singing on songwriter's demos. Eventually she became the receptionist at the company. At any company, the
receptionist has one of the best vantage points in
the organization. If they are observant—like
Trisha—they soon end up fully understanding the
entire operation from the bottom up.

As she explains it, "I moved to Nashville 'cause I knew deep down I was a real singer. But I also wanted to finish my education. I was raised to believe that whatever you wanted to do in your life, you should have a education first. I really wanted that degree. It gave me a sense of accomplishment and it helped me in business. Plus, it was a way to get my foot in the door and I wound up getting a job right on Music Row!"

Eventually, the demo-recording career became so successful that it wasn't long before she began doing that full time. "Watching all those people coming through those doors," she explains of her flight from MTM, "it gave me a lot of initiative to get off my behind and do something. So I did. I got some jobs singing here and there, and after about six or eight months I was able to quit my job and survive off of my singing."

While still in college, she met and married a fellow student, Chris Latham. "We should have just stayed friends," she says with regret now. "[He] was the nicest guy I ever met." However, it wasn't destined to last. It wasn't long before Trisha saw her passion for her career interfering with her marriage. But for the time being, Chris provided her with a great sense of stability.

Part of her education in the business came when Reba McEntire was in Nashville for an autograph session in a local mall. "I went up to her, and couldn't think of anything to say at all," she recalls. "I was such a geek! She probably thought,

'What an idiot.' She asked me 'Who's this for?' I
told her, 'Patricia.' I've still got that autographed
piece of paper hanging on my wall. Now that I'm
on the other side of the table, I understand what
it's like for [fans]. If they don't say anything, I
know it's because they're probably just nervous, so
I'll try to strike up a conversation with them to
make them feel better."

Eventually, the demo singing turned into background singing on a couple of critically acclaimed
albums, Garth Brooks's *No Fences,* and Kathy
Mattea's *Time Passes By.* In 1990 she landed a
recording deal with MCA Records, and things rap-
idly heated up for her.

She had begun working with Garth Brooks's
management company, Doyle/Lewis guiding her,
and when she went into the studio to record her
first album, Brooks sang harmony vocals for
Trisha's versions of his songs "Like We Never Had
a Broken Heart" and "Victim of the Game." As
she explains it, "Garth and I were already friends
at that point. And he returned the favor by singing and writing for my album."

Also on the album, lending a harmony vocal on
the song "Lonesome Dove," is Vince Gill. According to Yearwood, "I've always been a major Vince
Gill fan and the first time I ever heard the song
'Lonesome Dove,' I knew I wanted him to sing
those high harmonies. I remember walking up to
him the first time and saying, 'You probably don't
know me but . . .' And, he said, 'No, I know who

you are. I heard what you're doing, and I really like it."

Her first single, "She's in Love with the Boy" sailed up the country charts to land at number one. She also scored with the number-one hit "The Woman before Me" and "That's What I Like about You." However, the event that really catapulted her over the goal post was being invited to be the opening act on Garth's mega-huge 1991 concert tour.

Recalls Yearwood, "My background was in the studio. I was in an environment where you couldn't move, because there was a mike in front of your face, and you could not move from your spot. You weren't performing for anybody except that microphone. There were maybe three people in the studio, and you were there to sound good. That was the whole thing, the voice part. And so I when I got on the stage, my first tour was with Garth Brooks, this huge stage, and at least fifteen thousand people a night! I had no idea what to do with the stage. I mean, I felt so awkward." She soon got over those feelings, and began to stretch out and feel more confident in front of huge audiences.

"I was intimidated at first," recalls Trisha. "I didn't think his fans would give me the time of day. I thought I'd be playing to people still walking in or folks talking all through my set. I had major fears. My first single wasn't even Top 20 at that point. But they were so accepting and excited.

I got a great response, partly because my band is so great. Also we are in a better position than most opening acts, 'cause Garth was such a friend and he took good care of us. We weren't treated like a typical opening act. Garth was terrific."

"Looking back," she laughs, "it looks like I knew what I was doing, doesn't it? But not really. I was just flying by the seat of my pants. I knew I wasn't going to be discovered singing in some nightclub. I tried to approach it as a business and earn the respect of the people I worked with. It was a good way to do it. People in the music business knew me before the rest of America did. The songwriters knew what I was capable of through my demo singing and I had met producers as well."

However, Trisha's skyrocket to success took its toll on a couple of her relationships. First of all was her marriage to Chris, and second was her sudden parting with the management team of Doyle/Lewis.

With regard to the demise of her marriage, Trisha says, "It was like the best thing and the worst thing happening at once. We were already to the point where we were ready to give up, and once I went on tour, I was gone. How can you fix something when you're not there?"

She however explains, "Chris and I were great friends before, and we've remained that way. And, since he's in music publishing, he's one of the first people I call when I'm looking for songs."

"We got married too young," she interprets. "There ought to be a law that says you can't get married until you're thirty. Those years between twenty and twenty-nine, you're still trying to figure out who you are. I was twenty-two, barely old enough to have a clue."

The management split-up was a bit stickier. It was compounded by the fact that Garth's career virtually exploded in 1991 and 1992, and neither Doyle nor Lewis had the time to devote to Trisha's career needs. If she stuck around, she realized that she would always be the number-two priority at the company.

"A manager is very important to a new artist's career," Trisha explains. "It's like a marriage. Garth Brooks is the biggest entertainer in America right now and he requires a lot of time and attention. My career took off quickly and the connection that has to be there between artist and manager just wasn't there. How could it be, with Garth getting so hot? We had never formalized the agreement anyway. We were still checking each other out before signing any papers. Sometimes your gut tells you what to do. So those were the reasons I left. It had nothing to do with Garth. I talked to Garth about it and he respected my decision."

"When I fired them," she explains of the severance of Doyle/Lewis, "with nobody else in mind for a manager, it was right before they were named Managers of the Year, and I looked like an idiot. People were thinking, 'Oh, she's had a hit record and she's lost her mind.' I went for a month without management until I met with Ken Kragen, and he and I decided to work together. Then, I think, a lot of people said, 'Well, maybe she's not so crazy after all." Kragen, who manages Kenny Rogers and Travis Tritt, is one of the most respected managers in show business.

When it came time to return to the recording studio to work on her second album, the heat was suddenly on. "Nobody was really looking at me the first time," she claims. "If we'd totally failed, nobody would've noticed. This time around, everybody's expecting something from me, wondering if I can top it. When it came to choosing songs and recording, I tried real hard not to think about that and to do what we did originally on the first album, to find ten songs that we felt were strong songs, and to try not to overthink it, just do the songs the way they ought to be done."

She had made some valuable contacts in the year she launched her first album, so she brought with her an impressive set of friends and fans to sing with. Emmylou Harris joined Trisha on Yearwood's version of Harris's "Woman Walk the Line," and Vince Gill can be heard on "You Don't Have to Move That Mountain" and "Oh Lonesome You." Garth returned on the cut "Nearest Distant Shore," and Raul Malo of the group The Mavericks is heard on "The Reasons I've Forgotten" and "Wrong Side of Memphis."

However, the most interesting guest-starring turn came on the songs "Walkaway Joe" and "Hearts in Armor," as it was with the former Eagles star Don Henley. The connection came about in 1991, when Don saw Trisha singing on "The Tonight Show." He was so impressed with her that he invited Trisha to perform at his Los Angeles benefit concert to save the woods surrounding historic Walden Pond.

According to Trisha, "It was the opportunity of a lifetime to get to work with Don Henley. When he offered to come sing with me, I said, 'How about on my next album,' and he said, 'Sure!' " In 1993 she returned the compliment by recording the song "New Kid in Town" on the "Double Platinum" Eagles salute album *Common Thread: Songs of the Eagles*.

According to Trisha, "With Don Henley and Emmylou Harris, I kept hearing those voices and I'd think, 'Sooner or later I'm going to get over the fact that that *is* Don Henley or Emmylou Harris in there,' but I never did. It's pretty overwhelming to have people who influenced what you're doing and want to be part of it."

When Trisha's second album, *Hearts In Armor* was released in 1992—thanks to the groundwork that her debut disk provided, and via the instant hit single "Wrong Side Of Memphis," like its predecessor—it too was certified "Platinum." The album itself was a huge critical smash. *Rolling Stone* magazine proclaimed, "The country girl is now a dazzling beauty . . . Yearwood has the potential for a long, significant career." *Newsweek* glowed, "Hearty and lustrous . . . the most powerful performance Nashville has seen from a woman in years." And, *The Los Angeles Times* called it "One of the most absorbing country albums of the Garth era!"

Suddenly, Trisha was all over the place. That same year she was also featured on the hit soundtrack album from the movie *Honeymoon in Las Vegas*. On it she is heard singing the Elvis Presley hit "Devil In Disguise."

It was on "Devil In Disguise" that Trisha first vocally teamed up with Raul Malo of the Mavericks. She had met the group at a Country Radio Seminar, and became close with the band. "I got to be friends with them," she explains. "It started out just as a bunch of us hanging out at somebody's house for dinner and later on, just like everybody used to do, we'd get out guitars and sing around the table. Somehow our voices blended like we had been singing together for a long time."

Not only did she end up with a band full of friends, and a new singing partner, but she also fell in love with the group's bass player, Robert Reynolds. "Well, my love life is very limited," she explains, "because I'm never home. But 'yes,' I am seeing Robert Reynolds. And I don't know, who knows? The thing is that we're both launching a career, and I predict The Mavericks are going to be big. Hopefully, they'll get the sales and success they deserve because critically they've been acclaimed and they are incredible. I've never been one to endorse something I didn't really believe in. But it is hard, to be truthful — we're both on the road. We've been lucky that our time off has coincided so far, enough so we see each other once a month. It's kind of hard to develop a relationship when you're both so busy."

Via her connection with Don Henley, Trisha's second album started drawing interest from Eagles fans. Suddenly, there was a whole new audience of pop and rock music fans checking out her music, and coming to her concerts. "It's amazing," she proclaims, "but I didn't think about it — this whole new audience when I made my debut. I didn't ever wonder where this is going to go with the audience who never used to listen to country. I mean, this is just my brand of country music. It's a combination of a bunch of stuff and if it appeals to people who don't normally listen to country artists, that's great. The more the better! I'm not trying to consciously go in a different direction. Like with this album, I didn't say 'Okay, let's get a little bit more of those teenagers we didn't get with the first album.' But I think it's in the songs themselves. I think more people are paying attention to country, so people are going to be more apt to check it out."

Analyzing her music, Trisha claims, "My lyrics are geared to the independent woman. I made a record that was me. It falls into the country-music category, but if I'd made it fifteen years ago, I don't know if it would have. I listen to Linda Ronstadt's old pop albums, and they're as country as my music."

As part of the whole "new traditionalist" movement sweeping Nashville, Yearwood says, "A lot of country people are coming out now who weren't influenced so much by George Jones, Johnny Cash and Merle Haggard, as much as by James Taylor, Dan Fogelberg, and Linda Ronstadt."

One of the most dramatic differences in Trisha's first and second albums can be seen on the cover photos. On the *Trisha Yearwood* album, the singer is seen with curly hair in a blue denim shirt, leaning against a wall, looking as though she is standing in front of a Tastee Freeze drive-in, somewhere in a small town. In contrast, on the cover of *Hearts In Armor,* Trisha is depicted with free-flowing curl-free hair, looking chic enough to be the superstar subject of a Blackglama Mink advertisement.

The cover of *The Song Remembers When* combines the glamour of her second album with the "down home" look of the debut disc. On it, Trisha is beautifully made-up, and photographed hugging a bouquet of huge yellow sunflowers. The effect is perfect: a little bit country and a whole lot of "glam."

The whole glamour routine was magnified when

Revlon Cosmetics signed Trisha to a huge ad campaign for their Wild Heart perfume. Revlon's Cecil Canale explains the reason for signing Yearwood, claiming that it was her music's "depth of emotion and her special beauty." The Revlon representatives brought to the photo sessions several glamorous outfits, yet it was an item from Yearwood's own closet that she ended up wearing. Appearing in the print and TV ads in her own red-sequined jacket, Trisha said, "It was nice to confirm that we're from Nashville, but we can come up with some pretty good stuff!"

Through her powerful singing, and her own personal determination, it is clear that Trisha Yearwood is around for a truly eventful career path. "Country music is a business," she states, with both of her feet planted clearly on firm ground. "I'm the head of a corporation, and my name is the bottom line. Even now, I spend one and a half to two hours a day singing, and the rest of the time is the business. Gone are the days of artists totally neglecting the business side and getting taken for a ride."

Well, the only ride that Trisha is about to take is heading upward. She has already appeared in the film *The Thing Called Love,* portraying herself. That's sometimes how red-hot movie careers can begin. She isn't likely to end up the "Victim of the Game." Trisha is more apt to end up as a superstar Chairman of the Board instead. For her, big things have already been happening, but this is only the beginning of a long and glorious singing career. She's spunky, chic, strong, beautiful and determined — and that's what we like about her!

Chapter Four
Lorrie Morgan

If each of the women in this book were to have individual titles, then Lorrie Morgan would have to be nicknamed "country's sex symbol." Sexy, chic, soignée, sizzling, seductive, beautiful, she is likely to arrive at a public event looking more like a glamorous picture-perfect movie star than like a country singer. What Sharon Stone is to Hollywood, Lorrie Morgan is to Nashville.

To call her a "sex symbol" in no way suggests that Lorrie is a case of style over substance. Quite the opposite. She may possess the added dimension of physical beauty, but one listening to any of her "Gold" and "Platinum" albums, and there is no question that Ms. Morgan has the vocal chops to become a recording star—sight unseen. Her string of hits includes some of the most passionately exciting songs in 1990s country music. Her expressive chart-topping smashes include the rousing "Except for Monday," the lush and dramatic "Something in Red," the self-assured "Watch Me," and the snappy "What Part of No (Don't You Understand)."

To call her "movie-star beautiful" is right on target,
since in 1993 Lorrie made her dramatic acting debut
in the TNN original teleplay "Proudheart." It won't
be long before she has movie directors beating a path
to her door at this rate.

As with Reba McEntire and Madonna before
her, it was Lorrie's stylish work in her music videos that was the tip-off that she projects a true
incandescent "star quality" image when she's in
front of the cameras. It's clear that hers is a
multi-media superstar career in the making.

Recording-wise, Lorrie is already breathing the
rarefied air of the select few women in country
music who are selling albums into the "Platinum"
sales figures. All three of her country albums almost instantly struck "Gold"—and she's only just
begun her stunning turn as a bona fide singing
star. When she released her 1993 Christmas album, she recorded it with no less than the New
World Philharmonic Orchestra! This is obviously
one classy lady!

Like several other women in this book (including Patty Loveless and Tanya Tucker), Lorrie Morgan made her professional singing debut before
she was old enough to drive a car! If you thought
that Lorrie's stardom was a case of "overnight
success"—think again. She's been polishing her act
for two decades now.

Born Loretta Lynn Morgan on June 27, 1959 in
Goodlettsville, Tennessee, just outside of Nash-

ville; she was almost immediately dubbed "Lorrie." Although it looks like she was named for singing star "Loretta Lynn," it was a few years before the other Lynn was known in the business.

Her father, George Morgan, was a Grand Ole Opry singing star, so Lorrie grew up around the business. He is best known for his 1949 hit record "Candy Kisses," which sold a million copies. Of her father, she recalls, "He was able to be a husband, a father, and a performer. I remember days when he would come off the road where he had driven thousands of miles, and still have time to take us to dinner or just to sit down and talk. I try to do that, too. There are days though when I feel that if I have to take one more step, I'm going to drop dead or pass out from exhaustion. But even my schedule is nothing like his was. I get on a Silver Eagle [tour bus] and lay down in the back. I don't have to drive all those miles, like he did, to get there to perform."

When Lorrie was just thirteen, her father took her to the Grand Ole Opry, and she made her professional singing debut, singing the song "Paper Roses." Lorrie distinctly remembers, "My little thirteen-year-old knees were absolutely knocking, but I saw Dad standing there just bawling, and those people gave me a standing ovation. I thought, 'This is what I'm doing the rest of my life.' I thought it was going to be that easy. Little did I know."

As with so many performers, all it took was one little taste of success, and Lorrie was hooked on the idea of a career in singing. "It felt so good to see a standing ovation for something I had done," she says, still cherishing every moment she spent on stage that day at the Opry.

Her young world seemed perfect, until suddenly one day, George Morgan passed away at the age of fifty, and sixteen-year-old Lorrie learned what loss was all about. As a teenager, Lorrie toured with country great George Jones, and performed for a couple of years with a bluegrass band at Opryland.

From there, she recalls, "I started writing and got on as a writer at Acuff-Rose [music publishing], and from there I went on to be their receptionist. I did a lot of demo sessions during my lunch hour and after work. Any time they asked me to do a demo, I would do it, and finally I got signed to Hickory Records, which was owned by Acuff-Rose."

She released a couple of singles, and garnered a nomination as Best New Female Artist from the Academy of Country Music, but her career never quite caught fire. With minimal financial backing, Lorrie hit the road for an endless tour of country music clubs, sometimes with local pick-up bands of musicians unfamiliar with her music.

Lorrie had signed her first recording contract in 1979, but it lapsed, and she felt frustrated as her

her life disappeared from her life almost instantly. "I looked back at Mom," says Lorrie. "Here was a woman who had been with a man for more than twenty years, and their relationship after all that time was still a fairy-tale marriage. I thought, 'If this woman can survive after loving a man for twenty years, then I can, too.'"

It was time for Lorrie to pick up the pieces and carry on with her life. "I really didn't know if I was going to survive. I really didn't," she claims. "There were many days when I thought I was going to give up. But, with the two kids, I knew I couldn't do that. They needed a mother. That kind of grounded me. I did it for them. I had to pull myself up by my bootstraps and tell myself 'You *will* go on. You *will* continue!'"

With her debut album being certified "Gold," and producing five Top 20 hits, her path was clear. She went back in the studio, and produced her exciting *Something In Red* album. On this album, she teamed with producer Richard Landis, and the results were brilliant. She ended up with two huge hits with the singles "Except For Monday" and "Something In Red," and the album sold over a million copies—and was certified "Platinum."

When it was released, *Country America* magazine heralded that, "Lorrie Morgan is looking for new turf to prowl . . . she's developed into a top-rate vocalist who feeds on challenge and diversity."

Indeed—she not only delivered excellent country snappiness on "Except For Monday," she also took Little Anthony & The Imperials' "Tears On My Pillow," and rock group Journey's "Faithfully"—and has made them all her own. On this album she virtually ran the gamut from A to Z!

On the personal side of things, Lorrie met and married Brad Thompson, who was Clint Black's bus driver. They had become acquainted when she was on tour with Black. However, their union only lasted for eighteen rocky months. Lorrie swiftly filed for divorce, and today quickly comments, "I hope in time I can totally erase it from my mind."

Lorrie was recently dating Dallas Cowboys quarterback Troy Aikman, who is eight years younger than she is. She proclaimed in 1993, "I'm happier than I've been in years. I'm relieved. I'm not looking back. I've chalked [her marriage to Brad] up to a wrong call on my part and his part. I hold no grudges against him; hopefully he doesn't hold any against me. We can remain friends, we were just not cut out to be married to each other. I feel better about myself than I have in three years and I feel more in control of my life."

Regarding her relationship with Aikman, Lorrie acknowledged that her every move was being charted by the tabloids. "I have not felt this way about anyone since Keith. I don't want anything to happen to the man I love. And, I have a feeling that the whole world is watching." However Lorrie and Troy suddenly broke up in January 1994.

Her third album, *Watch Me* was released in 1992, and immediately began to yield hit singles, including the number-one "What Part of No (Don't You Understand)," and the hits "Watch Me" and "I Guess You Had to Be There." Again she had scored another "Platinum" triumph. On its way to "Platinum." Her versatility again saw her stretching from the charming ballad of childhood "From Our House To Yours," to the snappy "Watch Me," to a new country twist on the Bonnie Tyler rock hit "It's A Heartache."

Speaking of the song "Watch Me," Morgan enthusiastically explains, "It's a very fun song. It's fun to do on stage, it was a fun video to make, and it was my first experience with a real actor, Rick Rossovich, who was my husband in this video. The video actually ends on a very upbeat note. It's got a happy ending, and that's what I think of when I'm performing the song anyway, that it does have a happy ending."

According to Lorrie, "Most of the time, when I go in to record an album, I do all the sad songs one day and all the happy songs the next. I think it's very hard recording them, to switch emotions off and on like that. On stage, it's not as difficult because it's so fast-paced and you're kind of going on the audience reaction, so it's not as hard to do it on stage. But in the studio, I do all my sad songs on one day and all the up songs on another. I like the sad songs. I guess it's a therapy for me. It's a way of expressing my emotions. I feel better when I listen to sad songs. It doesn't make me sad—I mean, it does, but it's good for me. Now if it made me depressed, I wouldn't want to do them."

In the last months of 1993, Lorrie Morgan was all over the record charts. She was heard singing "The Sad Cafe" on the Number One "Platinum" album *Common Thread: The Songs Of The Eagles,* and on the soundtrack album from *The Beverly Hillbillies* movie she covered the old Ray Charles hit "Crying Time." On her Top 30 Christmas album *Merry Christmas From London,* she was heard doing duets with Johnny Mathis, Andy Williams, and Tammy Wynette. With all of this activity, Lorrie had all of the musical bases covered.

The big news however in Lorrie's career, is her acting debut in the *TNN* original movie *Proudheart.* She explains, "My managers and I have been looking for quite some time for something to pull me into the acting world. We've been looking for certain scripts and reading different things that have been passed by us. Either the timing was wrong or the script was wrong, and when this particular project came up, they had a gentleman especially write a script for me. So I didn't have to get so far out of character my first experience with acting. It was so much a similarity to my life that I wasn't drawn so far out of my own character to be nervous about it at first. I read the script and I was very moved by it and liked it and thought it was a very big possibility that I could do it."

The plot of *Proudheart* encompasses the dilemma of a single mother who returns to her hometown for the funeral of her father, only to find her life there in shambles. According to Lorrie, she really identified with the character she portrayed: "There's such a similarity between Sam Farmer, the girl in the movie, such a similarity between her life and my life, whereas we're single, working mothers trying to take care of the world, and mixed up in our emotions about who's gonna take care of us — I don't know, it just kind of hit home to me."

One of the most interesting aspects of doing this film, was the learning experience it was for Lorrie. "I think doing as many videos as I've done," she explains, "and being around cameras all my life, it wasn't like a shock to me, but it was a lot harder than I thought it would be. The hardest thing of it is not the memorization of lines, or trying to act, it's the hurry up and wait, getting the lighting straight, the sound right. It's really all that that wears you out. My supporting actors and actresses made me try and be just as good as them, and know my lines as good as them, and I guess from all the years of memorizing songs on stage and in the studio, my memory is pretty good."

If Lorrie Morgan had not become a country singer, she could surely have become a model. However, she herself claims, "I would probably be a cosmetologist. I love working with hair and makeup and stuff like that."

How ironic! In August of 1993 the National Cosmetology Association voted her the nation's hottest style maker. She beat out the competition, including competitors Demi Moore, Reba McEntire, and Hillary Rodham Clinton. According to the Association's Joan Schneider, "We love her hair, makeup and dress and look upon her as a role model."

Explaining her own "style" that everyone has fallen in love with, Lorrie says, "Another question that's always hard to answer is about my 'style,' because there's so many moods to me and so many sides. One day it is rhinestones or sequins, the next day it might be blue jeans and boots. It just depends on my mood. There's no particular, 'Okay: This is Lorrie Morgan.' I think that's been a problem with record labels and myself in the past. It's always like, 'Okay, let's get an image for Lorrie.' But there is no image for Lorrie. And as soon as people start realizing that, the better off they're gonna be. Because if they said, 'Hey Lorrie, we always want you to be dressed in this particular kind of thing,' I'd go the opposite. There are days when I feel like I don't look good. I think all women go through that."

Case in point—the photos for Lorrie's *Watch Me* album depict her glamorously clad on cover, and on the inside she is seen lying down in a wheelbarrow. Guess what? She still looks like a million bucks in the wheelbarrow! She could wear burlap, and she'd still be stunning.

Perhaps it's just a case of her happiness showing. According to her, "The years are good now. I've taken some hard blows and things like that. But I don't think it's been as rough as people make it out to be."

Well, if there's anyone who deserves to find true happiness—it's Lorrie Morgan. With her album's mining "Gold," her acting career in the growing stages, and her personal life buzzing with activity, we can be assured that for the lovely Lorrie— there's much more brilliant creativity to come!

Chapter Five
Pam Tillis

She's fresh, cute, fun, clever, quipsome, and one of the most dramatically exciting faces in 1990s country music. Amongst the latest batch of "new traditionalist" women in Nashville today, Pam Tillis is truly the one to watch and anticipate big things from.

In her mid-thirties, Pam's road to "Gold" albums and fame in Music City was not a direct route. The daughter of country-music legend Mel Tillis, Pam spent several years heading in the exact opposite direction from her father's established career and famous coattails, before returning to the music that was obviously ingrained in her.

However, since she signed a recording contract with Arista Records in 1989 everything's been coming up blue roses! Her first two Arista albums have both been certified "Gold," and have yielded such hot hits as "Maybe It Was Memphis," "Shake the Sugar Tree," "Blue Rose Is," the number-one smash "Don't Tell Me What to Do," and the outrageously amusing "Cleopatra, Queen of Denial." Up until that time, she headed west to pursue a rock & roll career, was married and divorced, returned to Nashville to become a successful songwriter. However, where she is today—as a star in her own right on the country charts—is right where she belongs.

Her father, Mel, is of course, famous for creating several smash hits for a different generation of country fans, building his own career on such hits as "Detroit City," "Ruby, Don't Take Your Love to Town," and his trademark stuttering singing style.

She was born on July 24, 1957 in Plant City, Florida; at the time, her father was twenty-four and her mother was seventeen. Her birth and childhood are chronicled in her autobiographical song "Melancholy Child." She reflects upon her childhood as a lonely and introspective girl. She attributes much of her restless personality to her mixed heritage—half black Irish, and half Cherokee Indian—blended with the Southern values she grew up with.

"I always had the sense I was different," Pam recalls, "It's a mixed blessing to have a famous father. I figure for every positive, there is a negative. It's almost completely balanced out to the point that I pretty much start in the same boat as everyone else."

Although she felt awkward and shy in grade school, she was once voted the most popular girl in her class. According to her, "They liked me from a distance. By the time I hit high school, I was looking for any kind of relief."

How did Pam spell relief? P-a-r-t-y! "I was your basic misfit," she recalls, "and a *professional partier,* and I think my temperament used to be much darker. I have a homemade ego—I didn't have much self-esteem or a strong emotional center, and constantly looked outside myself for it. I think some of it was genetic. The song 'Melancholy Child' on my first Arista album was drawn from early childhood memories of my mom, who at sixteen-seventeen was 'a baby with a baby.' "

Although she felt like a misfit as a teen, she herself knew that within her there bubbled a wealth of talent, just waiting to come out. "People might see me at a gathering and say, 'God, she's an awkward girl,' or 'She's not really a looker, is she?' But if I sang to them, I knew I could outshine any girl in the room."

Now that she has come full circle to become one of the hottest women in country music, she is able to look back on all of her teenage traumas with a clearer perspective. One of her major setbacks came in a Christmas Eve car accident as a teen. "The public tends to think of the childhoods of the offspring of famous parents as idyllic, and not conducive to what might produce a serious artist, but that's not so. It was extreme trauma that probably turned me around. I've always felt uncertain about my own attractiveness, thinking my appearance was kinda flawed, but then at sixteen I was in a car crash in which my face was shattered in over thirty places from my cheeks down to my chin. My nose was flattened, my eye sockets were damaged, and it took five years of operations to put it all back together again. On days when the weather's odd, I still have pain, and the ongoing surgical upkeep makes me self-conscious sometimes about the angles of my album-cover photos or my video shoots."

"I had my jaws wired for seven weeks," Pam says of the accident. Although she remembers that the accident "broke everything in my face," the experience only strengthened her resolve. Months later she was back in Nashville nightclubs, playing her own music on "open microphone" singer/songwriter nights. At the time she had a job in town as the receptionist at her father's music publishing company. In between calls she would come up with ideas for new songs to write.

Recovered from the accident, Pam finished high school, and went on to become a student at the University of Tennessee in Knoxville. Favoring rock & roll music over country, in between the day of registration, and the day classes began, Pam had already joined her first band. Of her short-lived college career, Pam proclaims, "I don't remember any of my teachers, but I could tell you all my song lists and the clubs I played up and down the Cumberland Strip in Knoxville."

In the 1970s Pam began her performing career as part of her father's stage act. Pam found herself as one of Mel's back-up singers, The Stutterettes, and she had her own two-song section in the middle of the show. Although she loved working with her dad, and her taste of the spotlight, it left her wanting more. "I felt like a novelty," Pam recalls. "I had a heart and soul full of music and to come out and do two songs was just awful." When she left the act to pursue her own star, her decision came out of frustration. According to her she felt "like being a little plant in the shade of a big tree. I couldn't grow."

Pam had a great voice even back then, and her dad recognized this fact, and tried to steer her into her own country music career. According to her, he always wanted her to "cut this song or do this or that. But, I just always had my own ideas about what I wanted to do."

First of all, Pam was more interested in rock than country. "He was really very pro country," she says of her dad. "He wanted to take charge of my career, but I always really rebelled. The songs he wanted me to cut were just terrible. In retrospect, 'I did the right thing, Daddy.' I'm sorry."

She ended up joining another band, packing up and moving to California. The band featured a jazz pianist, and the music that they played was out of the jazz/fusion bag. "It was really wacky," Pam explains, "but it was something I needed to do. I thought it was real avant-garde, but looking back now it sounds like Dolly Parton meets Flora Purim. I wouldn't take anything for the experience because I had so many ready-made opportunities that I could have fallen into for business reasons, and I wasn't ready. I was just a young woman making music for the sheer joy of it. It was a time to hang out, play, sing, and not worry about a record or the charts."

Although the band only stayed together for a year, the experience was great for Pam. "People didn't care if my last name was Tillis. I needed that autonomy for a while," she recalls.

She polished her singing style to the point where she recorded and released her own solo album on Warner Brothers Records in the mid-1980s. "I ended up making a real eclectic—some people have mistakenly called it disco—album. It was an album of pop songs, some harder-edged than others," explains Pam, "There was one country song on it, 'It Ain't Easy Bein' Easy.' It was a transitional work for me. There was no identity there. It was more like a portrait of an artist searching for herself."

Oddly enough, the search for herself had brought her back to Nashville in 1978. Although she landed several local gigs upon her return, the extreme frustration of being typecast as "Mel Tillis's daughter" began to get to her. "I would do these shows and just sing my heart out. People would come up afterward and say, 'We just love your daddy.' I would say, 'Excuse me. What am I, chopped liver?' It would make me so mad, but now it is like, 'We really love your music, and we love your daddy, too.' I don't care if they say that first, but it's like, 'Mention me, *please,* because I'm worth it, because I feel that I have something to offer.' "

Along the way she got married, gave birth to her son Ben, and got divorced. "I married the wrong person, that's all there is to it," Pam recounts. "It made it hard on me and my son. It's tough being both mommy and daddy. Any single parent will tell you the same thing. My advice for everyone is never to marry under the age of thirty."

Pam's parents had divorced when she was still a teenager, yet they both remained totally supportive toward her and her endeavors. In fact, both of them separately offered to let Ben come and live with them while Pam got her career on the tracks. She however passed on the offer. "I could never do that," she recalls. She was always one who did things her own way, and packing off Ben to one of his grandparents wasn't the way she wanted things to unfold.

Discouraged by her attempts to stand up and be counted on her own merit, Pam decided to put the performing career on "hold," and concentrate on her other love, songwriting. Her goal was to land a songwriting deal, and establish her own identity that way. She eventually signed with music publishers Tree International. She was an instant success in that end of the business, and she ended up having her songs recorded by such a diverse roster as Chaka Kahn, Conway Twitty, The Forester Sisters, Juice Newton, and Ricky Van Shelton.

Looking back at that phase of her career as a full-time writer, Pam quips, "Nothing wrong with staying home and getting mailbox money."

"The game plan was to write for a year," says Pam. "I was at the point in my life where I didn't believe in forcing things anymore. I felt I had been swimming upstream for so long. But I was completely foiled in the attempt to lay back."

When it was announced that Arista Records was planning on opening up a Nashville office to launch its new country music wing, Pam's name had been kicking around as an up-and-coming singer/songwriter to watch. She was in the recording studio working with the group Highway

101, recording a demo for the song "Someone Else's Trouble Now," when she was informed that Arista wanted to sign her as an artist. When she was offered the recording deal with Arista, it took Pam a bit by surprise. She had been trying to become a rock & roll singer for over ten years, and here she was suddenly offered a country album deal! How could she possibly say no?

"I beat my head against a rock & roll brick wall for so long that I guess some sense got knocked into it: that this gal needed to be a country singer. It was my destiny!" she exclaims.

"I was trying to avoid hard country," Pam explains, "And then for some reason, I just had a complete change of heart and started embracing it. It's the craziest thing. But hey, I always reserve the right to change my mind. I'm glad I tried all these other styles. It comes out to be Pam Tillis's style. It has elements of country but there are other elements. It all blended together to become something that I only can do."

One of the most significant things that had happened in the eleven-year interim between her father trying to get her to record country, and Arista's offer, was the fact that the sound and the face of country music had evolved. Explains Pam, "The new traditionalist sound was influencing me. It had all the roots of the cool country of the late fifties and early sixties that I liked growing up. It just started sounding good to me again. I got real excited about making a country album."

When it came time to pick songs for her first Arista album, "Put Yourself in My Place," she chose seven of her own compositions. She wrote the song "One of Those Things" with Paul Overstreet, and three songs with Bob DiPiero. Pam and Bob had originally connected as songwriters in the late eighties in Nashville. When Pam signed her record deal, she put a band together for touring, and Bob became one of her guitar players. It had taken a while, but along the way Pam and Bob fell in love.

"We enjoyed writing together," Pam explains. "One night we went out, but it was all really platonic. Bob had just had a number-one hit with Restless Heart's song 'That Rock Won't Roll' and felt like celebrating. We went out and had champagne, and nothing happened."

Time passed, and one night the pair found themselves having dinner in a new restaurant, when Bob admitted at the table that he had been having dreams about Pam and her distinctive laugh. Recalls Pam, "I looked at him, and he looked at me, and I looked at me, and I said, 'Now wait a minute.'" They dated for three-and-a-half years, became engaged, and were married on February 14, 1991 — Valentine's Day.

It was also in February of 1991 that the album *Put Yourself in My Place* was released. Suddenly, her career was off and running. Her first single, "Don't Tell Me What to Do" zoomed up the charts to number one. This feat makes her one of only four female country singers to hit number one with their debut single. (Pam jokingly refers to "Don't Tell Me What to Do" as "a theme song for the terminally stubborn.")

The album also includes the rock-edged "Maybe It Was Memphis," the amusing "Ancient History," and the sad saga of "Blue Rose Is." One of the most stunning cuts on the album is "Melancholy Child," which has a Celtic sound to it, thanks to Mark O'Connor's mandolin work. The entire disk is very lively, peppy, varied and exciting. Pam's voice is stirring, and expressively passionate throughout. One listen, and it's easy to see what all of the excitement is about.

No one was more excited at the outcome than Pam's father. According to Mel, "I tried to get her to cut this kind of music for eleven years. I'm not saying, 'I told you so,' but with the Tillis name, people just think country."

Suddenly, everything old felt new again. Pam found herself really loving the sound of 1990s country, and the fact that it had pulled away from the "my-man-done-me-wrong, and I-just-lost-my-job" kind of themes. Looking back on her own musical evolution, and comparing today to 1970s Nashville, Pam claims, "I just felt there was a generation gap for me with my dad's audiences. I felt out of place in country. It was a different world—until now. With the explosion that is happening in country music today, I feel right at home and able to sing just about anything."

She admits, "I could have just listened to everything my dad said—his intentions, of course, were good—and grew into this little instant career, add water and stir, and it would have probably been over for me years ago. Instead, everything is opening up for me now. It took a lot longer than I anticipated but I have no regrets."

Pam really appreciates the changes that have taken place in country music in the last twenty years. "In the recent past," she drawls, "I don't think there was a very strong woman's point of view in country, because women were still cutting a lot of men's songs. This is publishing heaven here in Nashville and there were only a handful of really great women writers. But Rosanne Cash pioneered things for women country writers, and now we have alternative artists like Pam Rose and Mary Ann Kennedy. My influences were George Jones and the country-style Rolling Stones, but I stayed out of country in the sixties and seventies because it seemed like country was ashamed of itself, like it was apologetic and wanted to be pop. But now it's the last bastion of song with melodies and lack of artifice."

In the liner notes of her debut Arista album, Pam wrote, "First I'd like to thank ahead of time, everyone responsible for making this my first 'Gold' album." Well, guess what? — she predicted it correctly. The only way to follow up one "Gold" album — is with another one. So, when she came back in the studio, she did it again. This time around, the results were even more impressive. *Homeward Looking Angel* certainly lived up to the promise that its predecessor foretold.

Explaining some of her influences on her second album, Pam proclaimed, "I like it all: rockabilly, honky tonk, Celtic folk. Even on something that might be bluegrass, you're going to hear some soul licks and on some of the more progressive things, there's definitely some twang because it's all part of who and what I am."

Pam has a very funny sense of humor, and she often makes more jokes about herself than anyone else. "I've had more exposure than Cher's tattoos," she laughs. On stage she jokes that her American Indian name is "Running Mascara." Her sense of humor really comes through on her hit "Cleopatra, Queen Of Denial," in which she justifies her love for a man who can't afford to buy her a ring, in spite of the fact that he just bought himself a new pick-up truck.

Also on the *Homeward Looking Angel* album are the hits "Shake The Sugar Tree," "Do You

Know Where Your Man Is" and "Let That Pony Run," plus the rousing "Rough and Tumble Heart," and the poignant title cut. Clearly, Pam Tillis is here to stay!

Explaining one of the songs on her second album, Pam says, "Let's face it, women don't always act with men the way we would *ideally*. I have a song on the [1993] album called 'How Gone Is Goodbye.' People're always cutting songs where the guy screwed up, and this is one about a woman who made a mistake. There's a cool guy in the song and she took him for granted. Now, somebody who's thinking too hard may say, 'Wait a minute, Pam! Is this girl crawling back to this guy?' The answer is 'No.' But to me, if you're writing honestly about real-life situations, you're making a valid statement."

The critics have been touting her as the next big thing. *USA Today* proclaimed, "This second-generation singer/songwriter is turning out some of today's hippest contemporary songs." *Music Row* newspaper predicted, "She may just be the greatest female country singer of her generation." *Rolling Stone* pointed out that she "add[s] a smart, aggressive personality to country classicism." And, *Billboard* glowed, "Tillis demonstrates again that she is one of the best female singers in the business."

Suddenly Pam is right in the middle of all of the movers and shakers in 1990s Nashville. When country legend George Jones recorded the song "I Don't Need Your Rockin' Chair," Pam joined Alan Jackson, Travis Tritt, Mark Chesnutt, Joe Diffie, Patty Loveless and Clint Black as a guest star on the show. When Dolly Parton recorded her song "Romeo" with several guest stars, Pam joined Billy Ray Cyrus, Tanya Tucker, and Mary-Chapin Carpenter. It's kind of like no party is complete without Pam!

It's funny how Pam had to go as far away from country music as she could, to end up right in the center of it. It is kind of like Dorothy getting to come home from Oz. "I finally started figuring life out," Pam claims. "Growing up made me realize I'm not gonna live forever. If you got dreams and you're serious about 'em, you better knuckle down and give it all you got 'cause time is finite and that's what people in their twenties don't realize. They think you've got all the time in the world. Growing up for me made me more focused and I now get an immense amount of pleasure from putting myself into my career without distraction. I'm having more fun now than I ever had partying and carrying on. I love what I do! It's like before I had this emptiness that I was trying to fill up."

The last five years have really filled Pam up with the kind of happiness and self-confidence that she felt was lacking in her childhood. According to her, "Music is my saving grace. You know, if you get enough people telling you that you are good at something, you start building self-esteem. Part of it, too, is the desire to live up to that. You say, 'They think I'm great.' Okay, I'll show them. I'll be wonderful." Well, it looks like Pam Tillis has become exactly that!

Chapter Six
Mary-Chapin Carpenter

Mary-Chapin Carpenter is as much rock & roll as she is country. Her music is as likely to feature a classical-sounding double bass as it is to have a twanging pedal steel guitar. She could just as likely be on stage at a smoky folk club on Bleecker Street, at a folk festival in Teluride — a Western bar in Tucson, or at Radio City Music Hall. Her lyrics are more apt to sing the praises of personal activism ("I Take My Chances"), to recall a bittersweet memory ("Only a Dream"), or illuminate sexist bigotry ("He Thinks He'll Keep Her"), as they are to "get down" and party ("Down at the Twist and Shout.")

She is country's town crier of a female singer/songwriter. She has the ability to get to the heart of a matter, and to look a problem right in the eye. She is intelligent, sharp, hip, motivated and wise beyond her thirty-something years. Her appearance is stylish, but no-nonsense. Her social consciousness fuels her art, and her passion is genuine and true. Along with Suzy Bogguss and Kathy Mattea, Mary-Chapin Carpenter represents the folk side of today's country. Her vision focuses on small details like an old friend of a fading garment ("This Shirt"), or a locale which to most people is but a blur on the interstate highway ("This Town.")

Mary-Chapin Carpenter is a pure visionary whose songs make the listener listen, feel, see, and think. Don't look for any beer-drinkin' bawdy bar songs. This woman is country music's conscience, and everyone is gladly listening to what she has to say.

An unlikely country star, she lives not in Nashville, but in suburban Washington, D.C. Riding high on the success of brilliant fourth album, *Come On, Come On,* she has a nice collection of award trophies on her bookcase to look at—just in case she wakes up in the morning and wonders if her current turn of stardom is all but a dream within a dream.

Thus far she has won the Academy Of Country Music award for Top New Female Vocalist in 1990, a 1992 Grammy in the Best Female Country Performance category for her hit "Down at the Twist and Shout," a 1993 Grammy Award for "Passionate Kisses," and an Academy Of Country Music award as Female Vocalist of the Year in 1993. Her third and fourth albums have been certified "Gold," and the latest one, *Come On, Come On* is "Platinum." Still, personal fame is a hard concept to believe for Carpenter. She had better get used to it, because there are a lot of people out there just discovering her very intimate and socially conscious work.

Mary-Chapin Carpenter was born in Princeton, New Jersey. She had two older sisters, and one younger one. Her parents were both very creative people who were self-motivated. Bowie, her mother, had a job working at a private school. Chapin, her father, worked for *Life* magazine. For two years the family lived in Tokyo, when Chapin was transferred there to work on the Japanese edition of the publication. Finally, when they moved back to the United States, the family settled in the Washington, D.C. area, in 1974.

Music was always a creative outlet for Mary. "Mom loves opera, Dad loves jazz, my sisters had all the groovy albums and all the Broadway show albums. I liked what they liked." She started teaching herself to play the guitar as a girl. The guitar itself was left over from what Carpenter laughingly calls "the Great Folk Music Scare" of the 1960s. According to her, "I remember being in the second grade and playing 'Cielito Lindo' in the school play."

Following high school, Mary-Chapin took a year off just to travel around, and the following year enrolled at Brown University in Providence, Rhode Island. During the summer of 1977, she got on stage for the first time to try her hand at performing. It was her father who heard her in her room night after night playing guitar and singing by herself. According to Mary-Chapin, "He said, 'There's a bar down the street, they have open mike sessions, why don't you go out and play at one of those things?' That was the first time it occurred to me, frankly." Although she confesses that she wanted to throw up right before she took the stage that night at Gallagher's Bar, she ended up hooked on the experience.

It wasn't long before she got over her shyness, and decided to do more than just show up on open mike nights at one of the clubs she had been performing in. "One night I got my courage up and I walked up to the show host and asked if I could have a job," she explains. "That's what I did every summer during my college years. I felt like I'd become part of a supportive community."

She earned her degree at Ivy League Brown University, majoring in American Civilization. During each of her summers off, she sang and played guitar in small clubs to earn some extra money. Her sets at the time consisted of new interpretations of other people's songs, peppered with original compositions of her own. "After graduation from college, I was thinking, 'Well, I'm going to do something with this degree and get a real job.' "

Instead of spending her days perusing the want ads, she found herself spending her nights in the bars she was playing music in, and inadvertently drinking more than she should. After several months, her drinking started to get a little out of control. "I had a big problem," she confesses. "It was awful. I had to make a life-style change in a drastic way. It's still so painful to me to think about how I was."

To break the chain, Mary-Chapin changed her schedule, and got out of the night-owl scene for a while. She dusted herself off, put on a nice businesslike outfit and began to pound the pavement, looking for a nice little nine-to-five job. However, whenever she was offered one, she freaked out. Something inside her told her that she didn't belong behind a desk.

"I remember making a decision to go back into music," she explains. Her days of playing for free, and hanging out drinking between sets had to go. She set new parameters for herself, and began insisting that she be allowed to perform her own original material only. However, by 1983 she realized that at $40 a night in clubs, she was never going to be able to support herself. She broke down and took a job as an administrative assistant for a D.C. philanthropic group.

Along the way she became a big local hit, and in 1986 racked up several "Whammies" (Washington Area Music Awards) for her club performances. Later that year she began to book time in a friend's basement recording studio. The friend was producer/accompanist John Jennings, and the results were a stirring mix of countryized folk/rock. "It was done by a very patchwork process," she explains. "Whenever I had some money, I'd call up the guys in the band and say, 'C'mon, I wanta record this song,' and we'd all get together in John Jennings's basement. It was just going to be a tape to sell at Gallagher's."

Another friend, Tom Carrico, ended up representing Mary-Chapin Carpenter as her manager, and he was so impressed with the tape she produced, that he began to shop around for a recording deal for her. That tape became her first album for Columbia Records, 1987s *Hometown Girl*.

"The first album was a real labor of love. It was very unself-conscious and had no commercial pretensions whatsoever," she claims. "Then it ended up being bought! I was really very much surprised. It had a different life then, in that it was thrown into this commercial spectrum and was required to be something it wasn't. But it made me a lot of friends. If it weren't for acoustic music radio shows and college and public radio, it never would have seen the light of day."

One of the things that amazed her the most about her record deal was the fact that it was the Nashville division of Columbia that signed her. Although she has a bit of a Nashvillesque twang in her delivery, she never thought that the country-music world would embrace her first. After all, she has more in common with Janis Ian than she does with Tammy Wynette, but the sound of country music had broadened enough to embrace its rock side, and its folk side.

"In another era, I probably wouldn't be considered a country artist. Country has changed in the last few years to where a singer/songwriter like myself is able to find a niche there. I really appreciate that," she claims.

"As the genre has grown and changed, its stereotypes don't apply as they used to," says Mary-Chapin. "Clichés exist, but you have to realize there's a lot of us out there who aren't adhering to them. It's really about breaking down barriers. I feel a lot of women who came before me made it easier for me to be here. I think each generation can look to the one before it, to see why they are able to be where they are in the first place. And a lot of people I feel are writing, working and singing today who continue to inspire me on the regular basis—men and women. I draw inspiration and awe from men and women doing what they want to do."

Although Carpenter's career took off instantly in terms of critical appreciation, money and security are another thing. Signed to Columbia, for two years she kept her day job. She was thrilled just to have medical insurance and a dependable car in which she could drive to gigs. "It never ceased to crack me up when we pulled in somewhere and they'd say, 'Where's your bus?' People think, 'Oh, you got signed to a major label. You must be on Easy Street.' "

With her second album, *State of the Heart,* things began to come together. It contained her first string of chart hits: "How Do," "Never Had It So Good," "Something of a Dreamer," and "This Shirt." The album cut "Quittin' Time" was nominated for the Best Country Female Performance Grammy Award.

When *State of the Heart* was released, *Stereo Review* magazine called her "a songwriter of uncommon wisdom, clarity, and craft," and her tunes "music that is both commercial and intelligent, universal yet intensely personal."

In 1989 she was finally confident enough to quit her day job. However, her first instinct was sheer terror. "Up to that point I'd had structure in my life for so long that, for a while, I didn't know what to do with myself," she explains. "I felt like, 'Well, now I've got to write something every day; if I don't have something to show for every day, I'm a waste, a mistake, and I don't deserve this.' [country singer] Shawn Colvin, is one of my best friends, and she got me through the first two or three months after I quit my day job. She was living in New York at the time, and I'd call her up and go, 'I-I-I-I don't know what to do!' She'd say, 'Go to a movie.' I'd say, 'No, you don't understand, I can't go to a movie!' She'd say, 'Chapin, just stop it!' It was very hard."

True broad-based fame was the next thing Mary-Chapin Carpenter had to learn to make fit into her life. It was her next album that clinched the deal. Released in 1991, *Shooting Straight in the Dark,* was about to throw the spotlight on her in a really big way.

The album contained such gems as "Halley Came To Jackson," about the famed comet and its effect on one particular family; "You Win Again," about a bitter message left on an answering machine, and the wonderfully jubilant "Down at the Twist and Shout" which features the stellar New Orleans Cajun band Beausoleil.

Stereo Review claimed of the *Shooting Straight in the Dark* album, "Carpenter continues to prove herself a literate, affecting communicator, an illuminator of dark corners and a collector of tossed-away feelings." *Country America* magazine announced, "In 'Shooting Straight In The Dark,' Carpenter's marksmanship finds its target somewhere between the heart and the head."

When "Down at the Twist and Shout" snagged Carpenter a Grammy, it pushed the album beyond the "Gold" mark. Suddenly she had to deal with across-the-board fame. For Mary-Chapin this represented not only reward, but responsibility as well. "Success is feeling like you make sense of your place in the world, that you make a difference with what you do in some way," she claims. "You're not continually self-absorbed. You're aware of your environment. You are a concerned citizen."

With regard to writing her biggest hit song, "Down at the Twist and Shout," Carpenter says, "I always tend to be working on something. I was home maybe five years ago on a Saturday night and it was raining outside and I just started thinking about the club named Twist and Shout [a long-since closed Washington area bar]. It was definitely an attempt to pay tribute to the atmosphere and the special quality of the place. When I was writing it with just myself and my guitar it had sort of a driving acoustic rhythm. The impact of Beausoleil on the track was the critical thing. It's not only fun, but really instructive for anyone who's a musician to try new things."

When it came time to go back into the studio in 1992, Mary-Chapin Carpenter again co-produced her fourth album, *Come On, Come On* with long-time collaborator John Jennings. She also enlisted the assistance of friends Rosanne Cash, Shawn Colvin, and The Indigo Girls. Again, Carpenter had produced an album of depth, truth and beauty, which garnered a "Platinum" certification.

Come On, Come On features the rousing smashes "Passionate Kisses" and "I Feel Lucky," and some of her most intimate songs to date. The areas she illuminates include a woman leaving a marriage in which she was more of a domestic than a partner ("He Thinks He'll Keep Her"), the rewards of struggle and attainment ("The Hard Way"), and the beautiful duet with Joe Diffie ("Not Too Much to Ask"). She also performs a fantastic version of Mark Knopfler's ironic "The Bug," in which she sings of sometimes being "the windshield," and other times being the squashed "bug."

When the album was released, *Time* magazine claimed, "With . . . 'Come On, Come On,' she displays a fully matured talent, her sure alto caressing a wide variety of musical settings."

Throughout the album, Carpenter makes her feelings, her emotions, her convictions, and her personal thoughts known. Beyond the recording

end of things, she puts herself where her mouth
is. She doesn't just speak of tolerance, understanding, and the evils of wrongdoing — she lends
her time and her talent. She has supported a variety of causes that are dear to her heart — like
Farm Aid, and Earth Day celebrations. In 1993,
when thirty-five stars of country music bonded
together to launch the campaign "Country Music
AIDS Awareness Campaign Nashville," Mary-
Chapin Carpenter and Mark Chesnutt were its
co-chairpersons. According to her, "It helps to
feel like you're giving a little something back. It's
corny, but it's the truth. It does feel like there is
some sense of merging between art and belief
and day-to-day life."

When Garth Brooks released his controversial
song "We Shall Be Free," Carpenter was one of
the most committed industry peers to come to his
defense. In the lyrics of the song, Brooks made
the statement that everyone should be free to love
whomever they choose. Several country radio stations refused to play the song. "Frankly, I'm of-
fended," said Mary-Chapin at the time, "and,
really taken aback that that message would even
be considered controversial. As far as I'm concerned, it's not even a progressive message; it's a
humanist message. It's a message about empower-
ing humanity and simply being tolerant. I mean,
what's next? I mean, come on! I don't know: if

people are resistant to something like that, we still have a long way to go, don't we?"

When Dolly Parton was recording her 1993 *Slow Dancing with the Moon* album, she asked Mary-Chapin Carpenter to be one of the guest stars on the song and video "Romeo," along with Billy Ray Cyrus, Kathy Mattea, Tanya Tucker, and Pam Tillis. Mary also sang harmony vocals on Dolly's song "More Where That Came From."

No one was more surprised and pleased about the project than Mary-Chapin. According to her, "I have had a few people sort of say things like, 'Gosh, Chapin, I was kinda surprised to see you in that video! It's almost as if I've created some humorless persona for myself, which frightens me. But I just figure, how many times in life is Dolly Parton gonna call me up and say, 'Hey, come spend the day with me!?' "

One of the things that Mary-Chapin Carpenter loves the most about being part of 1990s country music, is the fact that it is changing, growing and evolving. According to her, "It's not just as simplistic as 'My guy left me and now I'm sitting in a bar playing the jukebox.' The issues are edgier, and more compelling. Music to me is very brave and interesting, and to me, that's real life, and that's what makes me want to listen to the music. That's what makes me want to seek it out."

She furthermore states, "You can reasonably

argue that the most adventurous stuff is being done by women." She also takes a stand against the stereotypical image of a woman in country music that some people still harbor—all rhinestones, fringe and beehive hairdos. "The old stereotypes just don't apply anymore," she says resolutely. "Nowadays it has less to do with what you look like than what you're saying and how you say it." As long as Mary-Chapin Carpenter is in the forefront of today's country music scene, it is truly a more wondrous place.

Chapter Seven
K. T. Oslin

Country music was in a coma around 1987. It was a "limbo" era between the "Urban Cowboy" upsurgence of the early 1980s, and the revitalized "new traditionalist" movement of the 1990s. Totally unannounced, a plucky woman in her midforties virtually exploded on the scene and brought insightful excitement and a refreshing panache along with her. She wasn't an ingenue, a farm girl, a guitar picker, or any other stereotypical country songstress by any stretch of the imagination. She was a Manhattan actress who—in spite of the Broadway experience on her resume—always sang her witty self-penned songs with a country twang.

She didn't sing about birthing babies, doing shots of tequila with the boys, or any of those cheatin'-man-of-mine laments that Nashville was used to. What she did sing about was what it was like to suddenly wake up in your forties, wanting more out of life. She sang of her life experiences

(" '80s Ladies"), of middle-aged life's doubts ("Dr. Dr."), and of chasing younger men ("Hey Bobby," "Younger Men.") Her name is K. T. Oslin, and largely because of her, the perception of a modern country-music star—suddenly broadened. Due to her forceful entrance into the spotlight, the door was suddenly open for other intelligent singing/songwriting women in country.

With the release of her "Platinum" album, " '80s Ladies," people who would never have thought about buying a country album, were suddenly tuning in to her music and becoming Oslin fans. There were millions of music lovers who had done disco, felt lost in Top 40 radio, detested rap, yet longed for something fresh and new. What Tracy Chapman did for urban folk, K. T. Oslin did for country. She was mature, hip, able to laugh at herself, and with her songs—she was able to tell a story with clarity and honesty.

Six years and three albums later, K. T. Oslin is in another place with her career. With the release of her 1993 album *K. T. Oslin/Greatest Hits: Songs From an Aging Sex Bomb,* she is at a self-imposed crossroads. She is contemplating a more pop-oriented direction for her next disk, but her contribution to today's country music is very "au courant."

Born Kay Toinette Oslin, in Crossett, Arkansas, she had an interesting life from the very start. Her father died of leukemia when she was five, leaving her lab technician mother to raise K. T. and her older brother Larry. According to her, the death of her father set her on a course of emotional independence: "[It cost me] a tremendous price in emotional development, as far as relating to men, because my father died when he was still a knight in shining armor, and they should all be young and perfect like that. But in some ways it helped me not to rely upon men too much. To me, it was normal that a woman worked and paid her own bills."

Over the years, little K.T. had a succession of four different "step-fathers." The first one of them was in the transportation business, and the family moved with him to such varied locales as Mobile, Alabama; Lufkin, Texas; and Managua, Nicaragua. From Nicaragua it was on to Memphis, Tennessee, and eventually Houston, Texas—where K.T. graduated from high school.

While she was in high school she used to hang out at the most avant garde place in town, a coffeehouse called The Purple Onion. She drank espresso and wore black turtlenecks, and the Milby High School track team members dubbed her "Miss Beatnik." She studied drama at the Lon Morris College in Jacksonville, Texas for two years, joined a folk trio with Guy Clark, split for California to make a never-released Joan Baez-style album of folk tunes, and eventually moved back to Texas.

Back in Houston in 1966, the touring company of *Hello Dolly* starring Betty Grable rolled into town. When they got there they posted a casting call for two chorus members. K.T. sang the song "Summertime" as her audition piece, and "bingo!" she was offered the job. "That was a Friday, and on Monday I left for six months," she explains. "I didn't know what I was doing. I was just filled with — well, balls!"

She spent the better part of a year on the road, and then came into Broadway with the show. Her first Manhattan accommodations consisted of a sublet apartment on 15th Street, with the bathtub in the kitchen. "New York was just an incredible adjustment," she explains. "I got off the bus in my A-line skirt, with my matching luggage, my cat, and my perfect hairdo, and winos started spilling booze on my shoes. I thought, 'Girl, what have you done?' "

She spent the next twenty years trying to find her niche in show business. She portrayed a Puerto Rican gang member in *West Side Story,* had a small role in *Promises, Promises,* went to dozens of auditions, and starred in about forty TV commercials. Her most famous one found her cast as a woman who — while riding a roller coaster — is seen extolling about the merits of Fixodent denture cream: "A woman in my position can't worry about hold!" she exclaimed to the camera.

Recalling those days, K.T. claims, "I wasn't pretty enough to be a Campbell's Soup mommy or funny-looking enough to be the Federal Express weirdo."

She took a brief respite from urban life, and devoted two years to "doing macramé and growing tomatoes," outside of the city. After she grew tired of that, she moved back to Manhattan, totally switched directions, and shifted her focus from hemorrhoid commercials to songwriting.

When an old boyfriend offered to give her a piano that his parents wanted to get rid of, she gladly took it and began teaching herself to play again. She drew upon the piano lessons of her childhood, and advanced her proficiency to the point of being able to play the blues and boogie-woogie. The first song that she composed herself was called "I Ain't Never Gonna Love Nobody but Cornell Crawford." It was inspired by a memorable piece of gossip she read on a bathroom wall in a Due West, North Carolina cafe.

The funny thing was the fact that in spite of her perfectly modulated commercial speaking voice, when she was singing her songs, they came out sounding country-tinged. She explains, "They were definitely country. They just came out that way." The funny thing was the fact that she herself had tuned out of the whole country music scene at a certain point. According to her, she hated it "during the sixties, when it was all middle-aged men singing about drinking whiskey and cheating on their loyal wives. I didn't like the genre."

In 1983 she ended up signed to Elektra Records, where she released two singles. Neither of the songs, "Clean Your Own Tables" and the first version of "Younger Men," made a dent in the charts. When Elektra dropped their option on K. T.'s recording contract, they simply had a secretary call to tell her she was no longer on the label.

Not easily discouraged, she shifted her focus to songwriting, and successfully had her tunes covered by Dottie West, Sissy Spacek, Gail Davies, and Judy Rodman. However, time was ticking away, and K.T. at the age of forty-three was starting to feel like the gravy train had left her behind. Depressed, she gained forty pounds, and spent the majority of her twenty-fifth high-school reunion crying. "I wept on my best friend's shoulder," she admits. "She's got a kid and a house, and I'm thinking, 'I've never owned anything. Am I going to be one of those crazy old bag ladies who thinks she's in show business?' I gulped and thought, 'God, I've got to try this *one more time.*'"

She had to come up with a new plan. Her worst nightmare was the thought, "Oh, my God, I'm gonna die, and the only thing I'll be remembered for is a hemorrhoid commercial!"

According to her, "I was getting to the age

where for most people it is definitely over, and it
wasn't happening. So, I said, 'Okay, I'll go
around a different way.' " She dyed her brown
hair red, borrowed $7,000.00 from her stock-
broker Aunt Reba, rented a nightclub in Nashville
for a night, and staged her own showcase. The
last $1,500.00, she spent on a three-song demo
tape, which she recorded with producer Harold
Shedd. It took several months to get a nibble
from a record label, but finally Joe Galante of
RCA Records invited her out for lunch. They
began negotiating a recording deal for K.T. the
next day.

Her first single, " '80s Ladies" became a huge
smash. When her first album, also entitled *'80s
Ladies*, was released, it entered the *Billboard*
magazine charts at number 15. It was the highest
chart entry ever for a debuting female country
artist. With this album, K.T. virtually turned
Nashville on its ear. It was Tom T. Hall who
affectionately christened Oslin as "everybody's
screwed-up sister." She had definitely made her
mark, from the word "go!"

This all happened to K.T. when she was forty-
four years old. According to her, she was the
most amazed person of all: "People have come-
backs at this age, but they don't *start* at this
age," she claimed at the time.

When she released her second album, 1988's
This Woman, K.T. took her womanly wisdom to

another level. On the song "Money" she weighed the merits of love versus cash. She let the listener in on dishy girl talk with "She Don't Talk Like Us No More." Amid "Jealous" K.T. longed to be "the other woman." On "Hey Bobby" she extolled picking up a younger man in her new 4-wheel-drive Jeep, and with the demanding "Round the Clock Lovin'" she became the epitome of a woman in control of her needs. However, it is the poignant song of a love dangerously at the point of no return—"Hold Me"—that is the album's masterpiece.

When the album *This Woman* was released, *Stereo Review* called K.T. "an important new voice of the baby-boom generation." They called the album itself, "exhilarating, funny, straight-ahead, smart, and sexy."

Almost instantly, K.T. began to rack up awards. She took a Best Female Country Vocal Performance award at the Grammys, two years in a row, for *'80s Ladies* in 1987, and for "Hold Me" in 1988. "Hold Me" also won her a third Grammy for composing the Country Song of the Year.

Suddenly, K. T. Oslin was the national spokesperson for late-blooming baby boomers. According to her, "I don't think there is a forty-year-old in the country who turns forty and goes, 'Yeah, this is just exactly what I thought I was going to be doing.' Hell, I was forty years old before I had a color television. But I'm at the happiest point in my life now. I feel smarter, more in control of things. I was always waiting for my life to start. Well, it's started."

One of the benefits of success for K.T., has been on the financial side of things. For the girl who had lamented at her high-school reunion about never owning anything, she got to buy herself a house in Nashville with her new-found wealth. At long last, she had "made it."

She quickly found out that celebritydom has its plusses *and* its minuses. "Some of it terrifies me—the being recognized, the fear that I'll turn into a raging ass," she says. Weighing out the other side of the coin, she explained, "Young twenty-year-old boys come up to me and give me flowers. I'm talkin' real cuties. I'd rather be starting now than ending now!"

In 1990, K. T. released her third album, *Love in a Small Town*. Whereas her *This Woman* disk entirely comprised her own insightful compositions, she tried her hand at two classics—Ian & Sylvia's sixties hit "Love Is Strange," and forties chestnut "You Call Everybody Darling." Her own compositions included the ode to flagging resolve: "Come Next Monday"; a red-hot ditty about sex in the afternoon: "Oo-Wee"; and a bittersweet song about the end of a love affair: "New Way Home." Also on the album is the humorous bathroom-wall-inspired "Cornell Crawford," which was dusted off for this disk.

When success had begun to spin her off into the uncharted world of "stardom," K.T. quickly assembled an all-male back-up band, and she hit the concert road with a vengeance. She called her band Live Bait, and insisted that they all be good-looking. "I spend a lot of time on the bus," she claimed, "and I ain't gonna look at no ugly boys!"

Although K.T. represented the new look and the new contemporary sound of country music, she was surprised to find that so many people in show business were still mentally back in the "Louisiana Hayride" days when they heard the word "country." According to K.T., "Country was the ugly stepchild of the business for so long, I almost had to apologize for being involved with it. There was always that image problem. I can remember getting ready to go on 'The Tonight Show,' and I'd be wearing this nice Armani dress. Then, they'd drag out the Miss Kitty set and I'd ask why they were doing that. The answer was always, 'Well, because you're a country/western singer.' They didn't get it. I mean 'country/western?' There really hasn't been much 'western' music since The Sons of the Pioneers!"

For four years everything was going swimmingly well for K.T. — at least it looked that way from the outside. However, after struggling for all those years, and to suddenly hit such a tor-

nado of fame, her world began to spin very fast.
Life on the tour bus got to be a little old, very
quickly. Then, in late 1991 her doctor confirmed
that she was going through menopause. Suddenly
by the end of the year, she decided that she
needed to take a much-deserved break, to catch
her breath. While catching her breath, in rapid
succession — in 1991 her dog died, and in 1992
her mother died, followed by her cat dying. That
was the straw that broke the camel's back. The
indomitable K. T. Oslin found herself at home in
her bathrobe, devastated and depressed.

Discussing all the things she suddenly had to
deal with, K.T. pondered, "I got tired, I got
bored, and I got frustrated. I really did sort of
go to Zombieland. I've been in this business a
long time, and I think it just kind of caught up
with me."

With regard to the menopause issue, she explained, "In the past I had chosen not to get
pregnant. Now I didn't have a choice. I became
immobilized. I was like a big, dumb Persian cat."

Finally, in 1993 it was time for K.T. to come
out of seclusion. Discussing *Songs from an Aging
Sex Bomb,* K.T. explains, "It was something that
I felt I owed to my record company. It's not that
they said, 'Look, you have to do this.' They asked
me to do it. They asked me to do a pop project.
And I said, 'Well, I'm not up to a whole album.
I'm just not up to it. And, I can't tell you when I

Singer, actress, and all-around "Country Gal" extraordinaire, Reba McEntire. The daughter of a rodeo rider from Oklahoma, Reba is one of the hottest performers in show business today. (*Photo: Señor McGuire*)

Linda Davis and Reba McEntire performed their searing duet "Does He Love You" on the Country Music Association's 1993 awards. Not only did their smash hit rev up the crowd that night, but Reba's plunging neckline caused quite a stir as well! (*Photo: Alan L.Mayor/Country Music Association*)

Wynonna began her multi-million-selling solo career with a decade-long history at the top of the charts, as one half of the singing duo The Judds. Since parting with her harmonizing mother, Naomi, Wynonna has been stretching out into more rock & roll sounds. (*Photo: Randee St. Nicholas*)

In the past three years, beautiful Trisha Yearwood has become one of the most successful new women in Nashville today. Her hit songs "She's In Love With The Boy" and "The Wrong Side Of Memphis" have put her into the "Double Platinum" echelon. She is also a Revlon Cosmetics model. (*Photo: Randee St. Nicholas*)

Pretty Pam Tillis comes from a long legacy in the world of country music. Her father is singing legend Mel Tillis, and she got her start in show business as one of his background singers.

One of Pam Tillis' biggest hits is "Cleopatra, Queen Of Denial," but her own days of being in denial are long behind her. She is confidently in the winner's circle in 1990's country music, and she loves it!

If one were to give Mary-Chapin Carpenter a title, it might be "The Conscience Of Country Music." Her poignant and interpersonal songs cut to the heart of serious matters that deeply touch the heart.

Mary-Chapin Carpenter (right) gets the help of an all-star chorus on 1993's Country Music Association awards telecast. The choir (left to right) includes Patty Loveless, Kathy Mattea, Suzy Bogguss, and Trisha Yearwood. (*Photo: Alan L. Mayor/Country Music Association*)

Mary-Chapin Carpenter's singing career began in the coffee shops of suburban Washington D.C., and it has taken her to the top of the charts. (*Photo: William Campbell*)

Letting her hair down with the Cajun group Beausoleil, Mary-Chapin's country dancefloor smash "Down At The Twist And Shout" netted her a Grammy Award.

When androgynous k.d. lang first burst onto the scene in the late '80's she turned heads with her looks, and sold records like crazy with her distinctive singing style. Her smashing version of Patsy Cline's "Three Cigarettes In An Ashtray" led to her work with Cline's producer Owen Bradley, on the album "Shadowland." *(Photo: Albert Sanchez)*

K.T. Oslin broke all of the stereotypes of women in country music when she released the smash "'80's Ladies."
Not only was she fortysomething at the time, but her
insightful country singing told not of barrooms and
rodeos, but of introspective topics that made everyone
listen. To top it all off, she is an ex-Broadway actress.

Sultry Kathy Mattea is typical of the new breed of women in country music—self-assured and aware of the world around her. Her folk oriented brand of singing has brought many folk devotees to the world of country music, and vice versa. (*Photo: Peter Nash*)

In 1992 Kathy underwent risky throat surgery, and bounded back with new determination. To cope with stress, Mattea turned to her favorite pastime—jogging. That's how she keeps her fantastic figure. (*Photo: Jim McGuire*)

Sexy Shelby Lynne drastically shifted gears in 1993 when she released her brilliant country swing album "Temptation." Although she is just in her mid-20's, Shelby sings with the power and passion of a blues belter twice her age.   (*Photo: Daniela Federici*)

Lorrie Morgan is so beautiful that she even looks
great in a well-worn wheel barrow! Her sexy look, and
brilliant hits like "Something In Red," "Except For
Monday" and "Watch Me," have made her one of the
most popular women in country music today.
(*Photo: Ruven Afanador*)

When Patty Loveless began recording her "Only What I Feel" album, she developed vocal cord problems that only surgery could heal. After recovering, she found that she not only retained her voice, but it was stronger than ever. She went on to re-record the album with her new full-throttle vocals.   (*Photo: Victoria Pearson*)

Patty Loveless made her debut at The Grand Ole Opry when she was still a teenager. Her mentor all these years has been Dolly Parton. Loveless is known for the huge hits "Blame It On Your Heart," "I'm That Kind Of Girl," and "Hurt Me Bad (In A Real Good Way)." (*Photo: Chris Carroll*)

Carlene's 1990's hits "I Fell In Love" and "Every Little Thing," made her a bona fide country smash. (*Photo: O'Brien & Schridde*)

Carlene Carter in her 1980 rock & roll phase. (*Photo: Brad DeMeulenaere*)

Carter moved to England to record several critically acclaimed rockabilly albums. (*Photo: Brad DeMeulenaere*)

Her mother is June Carter of The Carter Family, and her stepfather is country singing legend Johnny Cash. Obviously she was born to carry on the legacy in her genes (or is that "jeans?"). *(Photo: O'Brien & Schridde)*

When Suzy Bogguss recorded the Patsy Montana classic "I Want To Be A Cowboy's Sweetheart," who could resist her? Since that time, she has racked up one hit after another. (*Photo: Randee St. Nicholas*)

Suzy Bogguss is one of the most popular gals in 1994's country music concert scene. Here she is performing at the Tucson Convention Center. (*Photo: Mark Bego*)

Tanya Tucker, in 1975 as
a teenage singing
sensation.

Tanya in 1976. Even
then she sang about
very adult topics.

In 1979 Tanya went
rock & roll.

In 1983 Tucker softened
her image, not her
reputation.

Beautiful Tanya Tucker, circa 1993.
After 25 albums, and a wild life lived
on the covers of tabloid newspapers,
she has more focus than ever before.
(*Photo: Randee St. Nicholas*)

In the 1990's Tanya has racked up one chart topping
single after another. Her recent smashes have
included "Down To My Last Teardrop," "It's A Little
Too Late," and "Two Sparrows In A Hurricane."
(*Photo: Randee St. Nicholas*)

Dolly Parton first broke through to a mass audience in the 1970's with the hit "Here You Come Again." (*Photo: David Gahr*)

Looking like Daisy Mae in Manhattan, Dolly's outrageous outfits have always been eye catchers. (*Photo: David Gahr*)

In the 1980's Parton fulfilled a dream when she became a movie star in "9 To 5." (*Photo: Brad DeMeulenaere*)

Dolly in the 1990's has returned her focus to her country music career. (*Photo: Randee St. Nicholas*)

Since her 1989 return-to-country album "White Limozeen," Dolly Parton has racked up a series of "Gold" and "Platinum" certifications. One of the cleverest women in show business, she is also one of the richest! *(Photo: Randee St. Nicholas)*

Dolly Parton (middle) is the hardest working gal in country music today. Her trio album with Loretta Lynn (left) and Tammy Wynette (right), "Honky Tonk Angels," was debuted on 1993's Country Music Association awards show. Her next trio project will reunite her with Linda Ronstadt and Emmylou Harris. *(Photo: Alan L. Mayor/Country Music Association)*

The "Country Gals" icon to end them all: the one and only Patsy Cline. How many of the women in this book can walk a mile in Patsy's gold lamé slippers? She is the best-selling "Country Gal" of all times, with her "Greatest Hits" album still on the charts—it has sold over four million copies.

would be.' And, Joe [Galante] says, 'Well, would you consider doing a "Greatest Hits" with some new things on it?' I said, 'Yes I would.' I feel like I owe Joe Galante a great deal. So I did it, but am I ready to jump on that [tour] bus? I'm not going to say that."

With regard to the title—it was obviously K.T.'s idea. "My title," she confirms. "I said, 'Do we have to call it 'Greatest Hits?' [Joe] said, 'No, what would you like to call it?' I said, 'Songs from an Aging Sex Bomb.' It just popped out of my head, totally off the cuff. I had not agonized over it for days. It just popped out. Galante looked at me and says, 'Are you sure?' I said, 'Yes, it's fun!' "

To spice up the proceedings, K.T. recorded three new songs for the album, and re-recorded her 1990 song "New Way Home" in a more "pop" vein. The new songs include "You Can't Do That," which is about all of the things you can't do in the 1990s—like eating bacon, and having spontaneous sex. "Feeding a Hungry Heart" is about middle-aged women overeating to compensate for a broken heart. And "Get Back in the Saddle" reads like a memo to herself.

According to K.T., "In my opinion—and I am very critical—the new stuff, being pop, brought out the pop characteristics in the old stuff. There's a couple of the greatest hits on there that sound like they could have been recorded yesterday. There's a couple on there that I think sound dated. There's a couple on there that I didn't like in the beginning, the way we did them. But, whatever, they're still on there. Basically, I think the old and new do go together very well on this album."

More than likely, K. T. Oslin is going to do her next album in an entirely "pop" mode. However, whatever direction she goes in next, her country fans are sure to follow. If Oslin were to analyze her own significance in country-music history, what would she like to be known for? "I hope that I helped broaden it," she says. "I know I've received a lot of mail over the years from people saying, 'I never listened to country until I heard you.' That makes me feel great, like I did open some doors."

Just because she is going to begin dabbling into pop music doesn't mean that she is going to turn her back on country. According to her, "Loretta Lynn said something very profound. She said, 'You know, it's easier to get into this business than it is to get out of it.'"

Part of K. T.'s career expansion includes film as well. She recently made her movie debut in Peter Bogdanovich's *The Thing Called Love,* which also features Trisha Yearwood and the late River Phoenix. Says Bogdanovich of K.T., "She is an absolutely brilliant actress." Obviously, all of that time on Broadway has finally paid off!

In her personal life, she remains happily single. When the subject of men is brought up, K.T. quips, "Katharine Hepburn had it right when she said, 'It's best just to live next door to one." According to her, "I'm in a wonderful place. I'm alone, but I like my own company. I have money. I can be an old lady and not worry. I'm content."

K. T. Oslin is a brilliant original. She is a legend in Nashville for showing the world that you don't need rhinestone jackets and cowboy boots to become a country-music star in today's marketplace. This is one super-confident and original lady of the nineties who isn't afraid to cut her own path through the wilderness. If anything can be said about K.T. and her unique brand of honest and truthful artistry it is assuredly: "she did it her way!"

Chapter Eight
Kathy Mattea

First and foremost, Kathy Mattea is an accomplished artist. The fact that she is a country star is a secondary concern to her. As much enamored with bluegrass and folk music as she is with country, her blend of these traditional sounds has created the strongest bridge between those two close-yet-diverse musical worlds.

After recording six country/folk albums, and establishing herself as one of the hottest singers in the business, in 1991 she drastically shifted stylistic gears. Her *Time Passes By* album beautifully but radically melded Celtic sounds and bluegrass music. The results were fantastic, but some of her hard-core country fans were perplexed. Although some members of her country legion were miffed by her move, she picked up a drove of new fans from the folk realm.

With her latest hit album, 1992's *Lonesome Standard Time,* Mattea pulled the reins back in further, and steered her rig back on the country road—producing two Top Ten hits along the way. She has a habit of traveling to the beat of her own drummer, and it has paid off for her both artistically and in terms of commercial success. While Mattea's idol, Emmylou Harris, is clearly traditional country, and while singer/songwriter Nanci Griffith is considered pure folk, Mattea has the ability to take songs by both of those women, and to make them uniquely her own.

Kathy is kind of an unlikely country star. Not only does she not have a single sequined dress or a fringed leather jacket in her wardrobe, she is more likely to be wearing a pair of Nikes than she is to have on cowboy boots. She doesn't sing get-down party songs, or he-done-me-wrong songs either—like many of her country contemporaries. The songs she selects are more than likely to be human vignettes about family members, love stories, tragedies, and valued friends. Her odes "Eighteen Wheels and a Dozen Roses" (about a retiring trucker) and "Where've You Been" (about two hospitalized elderly people), have brought her the greatest amount of success. Along the way she has racked up a Grammy, three Country Music Association Awards, and four Academy Of Country Music trophies.

While her albums are filled with guest star performances, don't expect Garth or Dwight to drop in on her songs. Mattea's musician friends who "sit in" on her sessions are more likely folk stars like Bela Fleck and Tim O'Brien, or bluegrass Nashvillians like Emmylou Harris and Mark O'Connor.

One of the most curious and talked-about aspects of Mattea's *Lonesome Standard Time* album is the fact that it was nearly the last album she ever recorded. Amid the recording sessions for it, a blood vessel in Kathy's vocal cords burst and she had to undergo risky laser surgery to repair the problem. She hurriedly completed the album before the surgery—not knowing what the outcome would be. Fortunately, both the album and her refurbished voice turned out gloriously successful. Not only was she relieved, but her fans—on both sides of the fence between country and folk—were thrilled by the outcome as well.

Says Mattea, "It became a race against the clock. I had to finish all the vocals for the record before I had the surgery, and I knew that if something unexpected happened during the operation, it could be my last album. I don't think I ever appreciated more just being able to sing. I savored every note."

She is a native of Cross Lanes, West Virginia, and Kathy's father was a chemical plant worker of Italian descent; her mother was a housewife who avidly read several books a week. When Kathy was awarded a scholarship to study engineering at West Virginia University, it looked as if she had chosen a solid sensible career that both of her parents found quite respectable.

However, Kathy in the meantime had joined a local bluegrass band called Pennsboro, and caught the "show business bug," and felt the draw of Nashville tugging at her. When a friend of hers announced that he was going to move there to pursue a songwriting career, he invited Kathy to come along. Without hesitation, she quit school, strapped her bed mattress to the roof of her car, and decided that she too could become a singer/songwriter in Music City.

"It was so clear to me," she says of her vision of what she should do with her life. "I was sitting there at age nineteen with a blank canvas. Why would I choose to do anything less than the most interesting and fulfilling thing I could do?"

"I was a waitress, a tour guide, a secretary," says Kathy, recalling all of the odd jobs that she took to survive. "I felt like it was my big chance to escape the life that had been predestined for me: go to college, get married, have babies and get a job. The only other time I ever left for anywhere is when I left home to go to college. I was an engineering major, then switched to physics and chemistry. I knew I never wanted to sit behind a desk and push a pencil all day. I would have been some kind of social worker."

For one of her struggling years, she earned $30 per session, singing background vocals on songwriter's demo tapes. Finally, in 1983 Mattea landed her still-running recording contract with Mercury Records. Her debut album, *Kathy Mattea* was released in 1984. On her first two albums, she claims she was still finding her own personal style of singing. Finally by her third album, *Walk the Way the Wind Blows,* she began to hit her stride with the Nancy Griffith love story ballad "Love at the Five and Dime," the chugging "Train of Memories," and the sentimental bluegrass title cut.

"Walk the Way the Wind Blows was the first album of mine I would go out and buy," she claims. To this day she remains her own toughest critic.

In 1987 she released her fourth album, *Untasted Honey,* which yielded the hits "Goin' Gone," the Tim O'Brien duet "The Battle Hymn Of Love," "Untold Stories," and the smash "Eighteen Wheels and a Dozen Roses." The latter song, on which Mattea sings of trucker Charlie who drives his rig for the last stretch, and comes home with a gold watch for his years of faithful service, somehow solidified everything for her. The Country Music Association named it Single of the Year, and the Academy of Country Music awarded it honors as Single of the Year and Song of the Year.

In February of 1988 Kathy married songwriter Jon Vezner, and the following year, she released her album *Willow in the Wind,* with the emotionally charged ballad "Where've You Been," which Jon wrote with a friend of his. Again she hit the jackpot, when the song won her a Grammy Award, and she was named the Country Music Association's Female Vocalist of the Year in 1989 and 1990.

According to her, "Where've You Been" was the song that nearly didn't get recorded. "I almost didn't put it on the record," she explains, "because my husband, Jon Vezner, wrote it with Don Henry—I felt funny. I didn't want people to think I was choosing his song because of who he was. It just happened to be an incredible piece of songwriting. You see, I was afraid I wouldn't be able to be objective because he was my husband, but then I realized I had almost gone in the opposite direction in leaning too far back and that would have really hurt him. I saw him sing the song in Nashville one night and the people were just breaking up, just weeping openly, and I thought, 'My God—there's my answer. This song should be heard!'" (Vezner and Henry also ended up winning CMA and ACM awards, in the Song of the Year category.) In 1990, Mercury Records released Kathy's "best of" album, *A Collection of Hits*. It went on to garner her the first of her "Gold" record certifications.

With fame finally attained for Mattea, it somehow became a dilemma for her. "I keep thinking how someone somewhere's gonna say, 'She's really no good. Send her back to waiting on tables.' And, I'll have to do it!" she claims. "I still can't let myself believe that this is really happening. I haven't yet learned to relax about it. I'm very uptight when it comes to that. It's one of the constant battles of my whole life. And I'm in a business where if I don't relax and just let it happen, then none of the magic will come. It's my biggest challenge. It's like peeling layers off an onion. I get through it on one level—like selling a record—and think, 'Oh, I did it, I'm really there,' but then there's this whole other level from a deeper place."

According to Mattea, "I've cried a lot at the height of my success. A lot of it has to do with the way I was brought up. My mother drilled it into me that I shouldn't forget where I came from. She said, 'Don't let fame go to your head—you have to be the same person.' So in some ways it made me afraid. I handle failure much better than I do success. Feeling like I deserve it has been really hard for me."

To alleviate stress, in the mid-eighties Kathy began to get into jogging. "Singing is a physical thing," she says. "Instead of singing at the top of my capacity every night and using up all my endurance, I have reserves. Running also helps keep my head clear and focused in a business where there's not much of a routine to anchor yourself to."

The natural next step for Kathy, especially after winning all of the awards, was to go into the recording studio and replicate the same formula of her last album. Instead she decided that it was time to do something different. The inception of the Celtic/folk album *Time Passes By,* came about when she became friends with Dougie MacLean, a Scottish musician. The further she explored the Scottish/Irish musical tradition, the more she wanted to experiment in that direction.

"It was a really emotional, searching labor of love for me," she explains. "And, it was real risky for me, also, because I knew I wasn't trying to make a record for radio. But I'd been influenced by this Celtic music that moved me in such a deep way. And I'd won the Female Vocalist of the Year Award twice, and I thought, 'Well, what do you do now? Do you keep making the same kind of records to keep winning awards, or do you try to see what other potential is there?' "

The album that Kathy produced, *Time Passes By,* is a classic folk album, which includes Mattea's haunting version of the song "From a Distance." She was so excited to be doing a different kind of music that she really put herself into "overdrive" to promote it to the press and to her public.

Although it was artistically fulfilling for Kathy, this new not-so-country Celtic/folk album wasn't everyone's cup of tea. "I couldn't take 'Time

Passes By,' " complained a review in *Country Music* magazine, citing, "the pompous, pretentious 'From a Distance' and the Woodstockey 'Time Passes By.' " On the other side of the coin, *Stereo Review* found it "Moving . . . more insight and emotion than story line — tapping into the inner life of the singer, the songwriters, and the listener." And *Country America* glowed, "Its delicate and quietly impassioned songs are perfectly textured for Mattea's rich, hardy alto."

Although she turned off some of the country purists who loved her earlier work, she felt self-fulfilled doing this material. Her enthusiasm paid off, and "Time Passes By" became her second "Gold" album. However, after five months of solid interviews and promotional appearances, she started having problems with her voice while in Europe. "During the last show of the tour," she recalls, "I went for a high note and it came out sounding like Joe Cocker. The next day I couldn't talk."

The problem was diagnosed as being a ruptured vocal cord blood vessel. Her doctor ordered her to remain silent for three and a half weeks, so the blood vessel could heal. According to her, "I went home, put on my Nikes and went straight to the lake." When she got to the lake, she realized that she was too physically exhausted to run. She also decided that she really had to stop pushing herself and her voice so hard.

Her vocal cords eventually healed, and in 1992 Kathy was back in the recording studio to complete her eighth album, *Lonesome Standard Time*. The album was to represent a swing back into the country sound that originally made her famous. "At the end of the [*Time Passes By*] album," she recalls, "my manager and I had a long talk. He said, 'You can be Suzanne Vega if you want, and go off and be a folkie and a cult artist, or you can come back to center a little bit.' I took about a month or two to make the decision. I finally realized that that option will always be there for me, but at this point, I don't feel like I'm finished yet. I feel like country music is my home and where I belong. When I think of myself in terms of being a folkie or an alternative artist, it's like a pair of jeans that don't quite fit." With that, she turned a corner, and headed back toward more countryish material for the new album. To facilitate the shift in gears, she split from long-time producer Allen Reynolds, and went with Brent Maher, who was famous for his work with The Judds.

When a routine check-up on her vocal cords revealed that she was bleeding again, her doctor insisted on surgery. She quickly finished her vocals for the new album, uncertain if she would lose her singing voice with the operation. "It was real hard," she explains, "because when I went in for the operation, none of this had manifested itself in the way I was singing. It was a physical problem that they told me would get more serious, but I wasn't feeling it. So I was facing an operation at a time when I was singing better than I'd ever sung."

Happily, the operation was a success. Physically, her vocal cords were repaired, and her voice was unaffected. To conserve her voice, Kathy has cut back on her interviews and promotional performances. "When it happened," she explains, "I thought it was the biggest gift. I was put in a position where I could still sing, but I was not allowed to do all the other stuff that doesn't have to do with music. As a result, I got back in touch with the music, and I got back in touch with my day-to-day life. I learned that not everything is crucially important."

When *Lonesome Standard Time* was released, it became a huge hit for Mattea. *Country America* claimed it was a "crowning achievement for one of country's most generously gifted singers." *Pulse!* extolled of Kathy's "beautiful voice, a commitment to developing her talent and an ear for quality songs, like those on 'Lonesome Standard Time.' " *Music City News* insisted, "Lyrically, this package is a born winner, as is Mattea's performance."

The album's highlights include the campy "Lonely at the Bottom," the clever "33, 45, 78 (Record Time)," the poignant, "Seeds," and the heartfelt hit "Standing Knee Deep in a River (Dying Of Thirst)." It is truly one of Kathy's strongest and most successful albums.

Kathy is so on target when it comes to selecting songs that perfectly suit her voice. According to her, "For me, the joy is finding the ones that really have something to say. And, those are the ones that live on for me night after night. When I get really, really lucky, I find one that keeps teaching me a lesson over and over again, every night when I sing it, according to what's going on in my own life."

It isn't clear whether or not Kathy Mattea is going to stick with straight country/folk music from here on in, or if she is going to go off into any new musical styles. "If I can have brought some class to this genre, some lasting songs, not been afraid to take a risk, and not lost my own self-respect or dignity along the way, that'll be a lot to look back on when I get to be an old lady," she claims.

No matter which stylistic direction she leans in, her true fans are sure to follow. With a beautiful balladeer's voice, Kathy Mattea has the grace and determination to pull off anything she sets her mind to. That's why she is one of the most highly respected women in country music today!

Chapter Nine
Patty Loveless

Patty Loveless is the incredible girl with two distinctively different country-singing careers. First there was the one she had at MCA Records from 1988 to 1992, with her old manager, and her old voice. Then there is the one she began in 1993, signed to Epic Records, and sporting her strong and newly altered vocal cords.

Sound like a country soap opera? Well, it sort of is — however, this is one that fortunately has a happy ending. But wait — you don't know the half of it. Patty's road to the top also encompasses a stint at age fourteen as "the girl singer" at The Grand Ole Opry, a disgruntled ex-husband, and a *National Enquirer* style scandal, the vocal cord problem she developed in 1992, the risky laser surgery she underwent to restore her voice, and finally her 1993 breakthrough album, *Only What I Feel*.

For a girl who struggled for years to make her own mark in country music, this album and her number-one single "Blame It on Your Heart" have been a blessing for Patty—who is now anything but *love-less*.

According to Loveless, "I just want to make music that people can look back on and go, 'That was a really good album.' Like Patsy Cline. Twenty years from now I want people to say my records were good." Well, anyone who's heard the *Only What I Feel* album will attest to the fact that she's being modest.

Reviewing *Only What I Feel, Interview* magazine glowed that "Loveless's voice sounds more potent now . . . Loveless is poised to become Nashville's next big star." *Country Music* called it "one of 1993's finest—and most important—works." *People* referred to her distinctive blend of country and rock by citing, "She's equal parts Linda Ronstadt and Patsy Cline." *Entertainment Weekly* praised her by stating, "Loveless increasingly proves the value of musical integrity—and passionate dignity." And, *Country America* proclaimed *"Only What I Feel* is nothing less than a triumph, good enough to be called, perhaps, the one album, cut by cut, that Patty Loveless was put on this earth to record."

Born January 4, 1957 in Pikeville, Kentucky; Patty Ramey was the sixth of seven children in her family. Her father, John, was a coal miner; and her mother, Naomi—obviously took care of all the children. A distant cousin of Loretta

Lynn's, Patty was the child who sang almost from the time she began to talk. She recalls, "I always loved music, but I was so shy that when my mother would ask me to sing for company, I'd go out in the kitchen and sing 'How Far Is Heaven' real loud, so they could hear me, but I wouldn't have to look at them."

In 1967, when her father was diagnosed with black lung disease from the coal mines, the family moved to Louisville, where he could get more extensive medical treatment.

In 1971, her older brother Roger, who fancied himself a budding personal manager, began driving fourteen-year-old little sister Patty to Nashville to pursue a career. When Roger got Porter Wagoner to listen to Patty's singing, he introduced her to his then singing partner, Dolly Parton. The next thing she knew, Patty and her brother were hanging out in the wings at the Grand Ole Opry with Porter and Dolly.

"Imagine being a little bitty kid and getting to hang around the Opry and their TV show with them!" Patty recalls. "Why Dolly used to take me into the bathroom at the Ryman and show me how to put on makeup between shows—and that really reinforced what a country star was! And, to this day, Dolly Parton is what country music *is* to me. Of course, then I'd have to go back to school on Monday, so it was a pretty different way to grow up."

At the age of fourteen Patty had her first taste of instant success. She ended up replacing Loretta Lynn as the vocalist with the Grand Ole Opry's house band The Wilburn Brothers. She was also signed to The Wilburn Brothers' publishing company, Surefire Music.

With everything happening so fast for her, it wasn't long before teenage Patty fell in love with The Wilburn Brothers' twenty-one-year-old drummer, Terry Lovelace. "At first, Terry was just this friend," she recalls, "and the next thing you know, I'm this silly kid falling in love."

In 1976, when she announced to her family that she intended to marry Terry, they flipped out. Her family so vehemently opposed her marriage, that Patty married him anyway in rebellion. "That's what really pushed me toward Terry. So many people had been making decisions for me for so long, I just wanted to feel a sense of freedom," she explains.

Soon after her marriage, she dropped out of the business, and spent years partying, drinking and drugging with Terry. After several years of life in the fast lane, in 1980, at the age of twenty-three Patty discovered that she was pregnant. "It was a terrible time, with just so much hurt and pain," she recalls of her decision to secretly get an abortion. Both she and Terry promised each other that they wouldn't ever tell any of their parents.

"I was frightened to death because of all this stuff in my body," Patty admits of her wild life-style. "The abortion was a decision Terry and I both made. We swore we would never tell because of the pain it would cause our families."

Patty went clean and sober, and in 1985 left and eventually divorced Terry. Once out of the marriage, she changed her married name of Lovelace to be spelled the way Terry's family had always pronounced it: Loveless. From there she began picking up the pieces of her once-promising singing career.

She had gotten on with her life in the intervening years, and thought that the story of her abortion was something that was buried in her past. Suddenly, in June of 1993 she read the tabloid headline that screamed out: "PATTY LOVELESS KILLED OUR BABY!" and ran a story quoting Terry. Although Patty is certain that Terry is still upset over the fact that she left him, and sold the story to the tabloid newspaper for spite, he claims he was duped into telling the story about his ex-wife.

"I wish he could just get on," said Loveless of Terry, just after the story broke. "I hope that people will understand and that I'll be forgiven. I told my mother before the story came out. She said I'd done the right thing. Imagine how hard that was for her to say. Her daddy was a Baptist preacher, and she grew up in a house where it was considered sinful even to dance."

Meanwhile, back in 1985, big brother Roger came back into the picture, again luring her to Nashville. He helped Patty to produce a demo recording, and garnered an audition for MCA Records. She was immediately signed to the record label, and began working on her debut album. Working with producers Tony Brown, and Emory Gordy Jr., from 1985 to 1992 Patty recorded five albums including *Patty Loveless, If My Heart Had Windows,* 1988's certified "Gold" *Honky Tonk Angel, On Down The Line,* and *Up Against My Heart*.

Patty's hits included the Top Ten hits "I'm That Kind of Girl," "Hurt Me Bad (In A Real Good Way)," "If My Heart Had Windows," and the number-one smashes "Timber I'm Falling in Love" and "Chains." Although she came close to major-league stardom, and she racked up several awards, she only seemed to rise to a certain point at her record company. After the *Up Against My Heart* album, she became unsatisfied with the efforts of her record label.

One of the last straws was the failure of the Patsy Cline inspired MCA single "Can't Stop Myself From Loving You." "I'd always been searching for a song with Patsy's spirit in it. When I sing it, I feel she's with me."

The time had arrived for her to make several changes in her life. In 1990 she fired her brother

Roger as her manager, and eventually signed with Larry Fitzgerald. "I can't say it was a mistake I made with my brother when I came back to Nashville, because it was all new to me. He was my brother, and I trusted him wholly," says Loveless. "Making that change was a real hard decision for me."

Dolly Parton was one of the first people Patty told about her decision. Dolly had gone through the trauma of firing family members in the past, and she assured Patty that business was business, and if a change had to be made it shouldn't rip apart a family's relationship. Parton put her thoughts down on a tape recorder, and sent a copy of it to both Patty and Roger. Says Patty, "I met Dolly when she was twenty-six and I was fourteen. She's always been a sister to me in the music business."

Next, it was time to make a decision about her record contract. In 1992, when three other ladies who were signed to MCA Records—Reba McEntire, Wynonna Judd, and Trisha Yearwood—each broke through with "Platinum" and "Double Platinum" albums, Patty felt that she was suddenly relegated to being a fourth place priority at the label. As Patty politely puts it, "I had one too many girlfriends."

It was 1991's *Up Against My Heart* album that signaled that the ball had been dropped by MCA. "I believed in that album with all my heart,"

Patty recalls. "I felt as though somehow it just got lost in the shuffle. I feel that album just needed a little more push than it was given. I was a little bit disappointed, but I picked myself up and I dusted myself off."

"When I got a record deal," she says of her contract with MCA, "it was the greatest thing. It was like that first love that you want to marry. You want it to last forever. Sometimes, though, after awhile, you feel the relationship start to change. It was like a marriage that I wanted to work, but it wasn't quite working out."

In the summer of 1992, discontented, Patty asked MCA president Tony Brown to be released from the contract with the company. "We spent a lot of time on marketing plans for Patty," says Brown, "but we weren't counting on three of the biggest female break-throughs to come at the same time she was putting an album out." Brown could see how unhappy Patty was with so much in-house competition, and let her out of the contract.

Meanwhile, she had also made a major change in her personal life. She married her record producer Emory Gordy Jr. in a tourist chapel in February 1989, in the Smoky Mountains, at Gatlinburg, Tennessee. However, they kept the wedding a secret until October 1990. According to Patty, "We kept it a secret mainly because I wanted to come across as a strong person, a strong artist, and get established on my own. I didn't want to appear wishy-washy. I wanted to appear in control of my life."

With a new manager, a new husband, and thanks to Epic Records — a new label, it seemed like Patty was ready to make a fresh start in late 1992. She went into the recording studio to begin work on her Epic debut album, when she noticed that something was very wrong with her voice. She discovered that she had developed an enlarged blood vessel — an aneurysm — on her vocal cords.

"My vocal condition was affecting the power of my voice," Patty explains. "I was not hitting notes as strongly as before. I was getting tired after singing a song four or five times. I thought, 'Boy, something's not sounding right. I'm not hitting the right pitch.' And I knew. Also, my husband, who produced the album, told me he could definitely tell the difference."

Patty knew that something was wrong with her throat, but she kept trying to ignore the pain she felt every time she sang. "I was beating my vocal cords to death each time I made any noise," she reflects. "It was scary. I was freaking. I didn't want anybody to know it was that bad."

One night she was on stage with Vince Gill, and they were singing a duet version of "When I Call Your Name." In the middle of the song, Patty realized that she had a real problem. She recalls, "When I heard myself through that monitor, I just about died. We came off stage, and I said, 'Vince, I'm so sorry. I'm really having trouble, and I don't know what it is.'"

She had just finished taping the CBS-TV special "The Women of Country Music," when she went to the doctor to have her throat examined. "The doctor said, 'I can't permit you to sing anymore until you've had surgery,'" recalls Patty.

"I was saying, 'I can't stop. I've just finished half of my new album, I'm on a new label, I'm going on the road for twenty-five days straight of one-nighters.' I said, 'I don't have the time, I can't listen to this,'" she claims.

Instead of listening to the doctor's advice, her first response was to argue back. The idea of "surgery" hit her the same way a concert pianist might react facing a risky operation on her hands. Fortunately, she didn't go to the doctor's office alone. "My manager, Larry Fitzgerald, went to the doctor with me . . . I'll tell you the truth. If Larry had not gone with me, I probably would have walked out of the doctor's office and said, 'Well, boys, let's get on the bus.'"

If it had been up to her, she might have blown off the whole operation, especially when she was informed that the consequences might be never being able to sing again. "I said, 'We can wait.' But my manager, Larry Fitzgerald, looked at the X-rays and said, 'We start canceling tomorrow,'"

Patty recalls. "It was an emotional time. I just felt a little scared. I guess it was God's way of saying, 'You've got to take a vacation and you'll come back better.' I had to believe that."

Then she was informed that one of her vocal cords had a blister on it that was so big, the doctor claimed that it looked like it was covered with blood. "When I heard that, I just broke down," she confesses.

On October 21, 1992, Patty underwent the surgery, knowing that her voice would be altered forever—and not knowing if it was going to be better or worse. Friends like Dolly Parton sent their best wishes to her in the hospital, and braced her for the possibility that she might lose her singing voice. According to Patty, Dolly said to her, "You'd better get back to writing, because nobody knows how well you can write. Most of all, just hang in there, no matter what happens."

With all of this time suddenly on her hands, Patty began to reflect on all of the changes she had made in her career—firing her brother as her manager, splitting with MCA Records, secretly marrying her record producer—and she began to wonder if her vocal-cord problem had been brought on by her own actions. "I thought maybe God was doing it to me for becoming this terrible person, for hurting other people," she admits. "Stress can make you ill. The past two years had taken a toll on me."

After the physically successful operation, it was still uncertain how her voice would sound. She had to remain silent for more than a month before they could test the results. Emory even taught her to rely on Morse code to communicate during those agonizing weeks she remained mute. "There were quite a few tears," says Gordy.

During her recovery, several friends in the business rallied behind her. Kathy Mattea, who had also had surgery on her vocal cords, was very supportive. Naomi Judd sent Patty a book of inspirational verse, and flowers arrived from Pam Tillis, Trisha Yearwood, Barbara Mandrell, and Emmylou Harris. She received hundreds of cards from fans.

Says Patty, "It made me feel better about myself. I'd been thinking I was such a terrible person. I'd put myself through all that turmoil. Above all else, I want to thank the fans for all the cards and letters they sent. When you can't talk, and you're using a chalkboard to communicate, you find yourself reading those messages over and over."

According to her, "When you can't talk, and you don't know what's going to happen, all kinds of things run through your mind. You get scared. You get confused. You get frustrated. A lot of times, I didn't know what to think."

More than anything else, Patty was afraid that the months of recovery would be poison to her career.

"Four or five months in this business is a long time. I didn't want to be forgotten," she claims. "At the end of November, I was able to start whispering. I had voice therapy and slowly started to sing scales. I sang a little around the house in late December, and then we went back into the studio on January 4, my [36th] birthday."

Since her voice had been altered, she had to scrap the vocal tracks of the songs she had already put on tape. "I had to go back and re-sing all the material we had recorded before the surgery. It was scary for me. It was really frightening!" she admits. "I wondered if I was going to sound right. It was little bit scary when I got into the studio and started singing the very first song. When the musicians got through, they came in and they said, 'Your voice is stronger and we can tell.' That made me feel good."

One of the songs she re-recorded for the new album is a cut called "You Don't Know How Lucky You Are" that truly put her through the paces. "I'm very pleased after going through so much torment. There were a couple of songs that were really hard for me. I thought I wasn't singing them right." she claims. "I was listening . . . to this song called 'How Lucky You Are,' and I said, 'Wow, we finally nailed it!' I was about to cry."

Amid recording sessions for her debut Epic album, "Only What I Feel," she made her return to public singing—fittingly at The Grand Ole Opry, January 16, 1993. On February 11 she was in Gillette, Wyoming, kicking off her triumphant recovery concert tour.

The new album was released on April 20, and the results were well worth the wait. The first song released as a single, "Blame It on Your Heart," zoomed up the charts to the number-one spot. It was official: Patty Loveless was back— and better than ever!

No one was more shocked than the head of Epic/Sony's Nashville branch, Roy Wunsch. According to him, "We didn't know how long her recovery was going to take, or what she would sound like. But having heard the rough mixes of 'Only What I Feel,' I was shocked. She sounds even better, now, after the surgery, than when we signed her—this project validates Patty as the preeminent hard country female vocalist out there *and more!*"

"The difference is amazing," claims Emory of her new voice. "Before, she sounded like a bird in a cage; now her voice is suddenly free."

Patty herself exclaims, "I'm singing better than I ever did. I'm a woman now!"

To jump on the Patty bandwagon, MCA Records quickly put together their own album, *Patty Loveless/Greatest Hits* for summer 1993 release. Listening to it next to the *Only What I Feel* album, there is clearly a difference in Patty's voice, and her singing style. She is more passionate, more determined, and her voice is able to really belt out these excellently chosen songs.

That was the second major piece of the jigsaw puzzle in piecing Loveless's career back together—the selection of material. Well, on this album, she really pulled out all of the stops to touch every emotion. From the first notes of Patty's voice on the exciting song "You Will," to the last plaintive lyric line of "How Can I Help You Say Goodbye," it is evident that Patty Loveless has returned to the top stronger than ever.

Patty has longed to break through to the big leagues of "Platinum"-selling female country artists. She may very well be there right now. "For women in country music, getting that 'Platinum' album is a big goal," she claims. "A lot of women have reached it, but Patty Loveless hasn't yet. I pray for a 'Platinum' album. There have been quite a few ladies now who have gotten one. Boy, if I could see a 'Double Platinum' album like Reba McEntire has, that would be something else."

Choosing the right material was a very important issue for her. She returned to songwriter "Kostas," who had given her "Timber I'm Falling in Love." He gave her the hot new hit "Blame It on Your Heart." According to her, "Today's country is a lot like seventies rock—like the Eagles—and that's a big reason for the new success with baby boomers." She further explains, "I was trying to pick out a song like Trisha Yearwood would do, or Wynonna, but it just didn't fit. The song's got to fit you." This time around, she found material that fit her like a glove.

The most emotionally wrenching song on the album is the last cut, "How Can I Help You Say Goodbye," which is about the loss of a loved one. According to Patty, "This song was hitting me so hard that I was crying to the point that I couldn't get it out. I was so emotional with it because I've been through all these situations—of moving away from friends to a bigger city; I've been through divorce and I have lost a parent."

The melancholy classic was inspired by the death of the grandmother of one of the songwriters, Burton Banks Collins. Says Loveless, "When we were recording 'Help Me,' I kept the letter the writer had written about that song in my purse for over a month. It was about his grandmother dying, who'd seen him through everything, including her death, and it touched me so much that I couldn't quite get over it. For me that's something different. I sing with a lot of power—and I remember being in the studio, trying to do these quiet, almost whispered parts and I kept feeling like I was trembling. But I think now, that's where that song comes from, so that's where the voice has to come from, too."

"I've been around so many people and heard so

many heartbreaking stories that all I try to do is take those lyrics and give them edge," says Patty. "As far as a real hard-core country sound—what I call 'traditional country'—it's hard for a woman to break in with that. When men . . . do traditional stuff, radio loves it. They eat it up. I want to reach that audience, and I think eventually I can."

Stepping back and analyzing her career, Patty is able to note growth—especially on the new album. "With each album, I mature more and more," she says, "and I learn more about how to get the sounds we want on tape. This time I think we did everything more aggressively; I know I sang harder than ever! But we also really made an effort to record an album where all ten songs came together and they really meant something as a whole."

Patty admits to being a very introspective person who sometimes needs to be alone. "Even when we're together," she says of Emory, "there are moments when I'll look at him and say, 'You know, I really need to be to myself. Just leave me in a room to myself for a little while. I don't get a lot of quiet time on the road. I'm never really alone. I even grew up that way. I think from the days when I was a kid my mama knew that I was different. I kind of liked to be by myself. If company would come over, I'd go sit in the corner beside the refrigerator. I was real quiet and would just sit and listen a lot." Well, if she is spending any alone time now, hopefully she is thinking about her newfound success!

Perhaps her very sincere and well-thought-out manner is the reason why Patty has the ability to emotionally draw her audience into her songs. Women especially identify with her music, and her message. According to her, "Today when I look at the audience out there, and I see the women out there, it gives me an opportunity to get to them—lyrically, when I'm singing, or to let them have the freedom within a song. It's like: 'Hey, this is me she's singing about.' And, that's what I love to see on their faces—them getting into the music."

Although her life seemed like a virtual roller coaster for several years, Patty Loveless is back on top, and sounding better than ever. As she herself exclaims, "I'm the happiest I've ever been." With her new label, her new husband, her new voice, and the hottest album of her career on the charts—it's no wonder!

Chapter Ten
Carlene Carter

Born into a famous country-music family, with an even more famous country legend as her step-father, Carlene Carter left Nashville to take a 180-degree turn in the opposite musical direction to avoid a career in country. Twelve years later, she came back to Nashville—after five rockabilly albums—and has found her greatest success with her two latest country/rock albums: *I Fell in Love* (1990) and *Little Love Letters* (1993).

Married three times by the time she was twenty-three, Carlene's legendary life in the fast lane is nearly as famous as her music! Today, substance-free, romantically involved with guitarist/producer Howie Epstein of Tom Petty's Heartbreakers, her ascension into the ranks of Nashville's newest and hottest stars is a reward after several years of struggling for a musical identity.

Her infectiously exciting music on her nineties albums is impossible to resist. In her videos, Carter is a cowboy-booted, mini-skirted, go-go girl/cheerleader who is so bouncy and cute, you can't help but fall in love with her. Her sound has always been a peppy blend of rock, rockabilly, and country. It's just that she was years ahead of the ballgame. She was rock & roll when rock & roll in Nashville wasn't cool. Today her career is red hot!

"I guess all the planets just finally lined up this time," she surmises. "I really do think this is just the right time for me, but part of it is that I'm a lot more focused. I floundered around for years trying to find the right balance of country and rock, which was always a dilemma for me. I couldn't really see myself wearing frilly little lace dresses and singing ballads for the rest of my life, which is what I always thought country music was."

Carlene is the daughter of The Carter Family singer June Carter, and fifties/sixties country singer Carl Smith ("Loose Talk," "There She Goes"). Her grandmother was the famed "Mother" Maybelle Carter of the depression era trio, The Carters ("Keep on the Sunny Side," "Wildwood Flower"), making Carlene a third generation country music legend. When her parents divorced in the mid-sixties, June married Johnny Cash.

In the late fifties Carlene met Elvis Presley — however she was only two years old at the time. In fact, Elvis was her babysitter! June Carter was often one of Presley's opening acts, and they remained friends throughout the years. Explains Carlene, "Mama was in New York at the same acting school as Elvis, and on Sunday afternoons, he used to roll me around Central Park."

The child of Nashville royalty, it would seem that Carlene would immediately gravitate towards country music—especially having Johnny Cash as her stepfather. "But they were just my family." She laughs. "And then here came The Monkees, and uh-oh!" As a girl she fell in love with rock & roll, and it would begin a lifelong pull in opposite directions between rock and country. She lists her earliest musical influences as including The Beatles, Janis Joplin, Eric Clapton, Ray Charles, Jimi Hendrix, and The Byrds.

Married and a mother at the age of sixteen, Carlene grew up fast, and lived a "party animal" kind of life-style. "Lots of girls marry at sixteen in Tennessee," she says in retrospect, adding the judgment call: "Everyone makes mistakes." She has a daughter, Tiffany, from her first marriage; and a son, Jackson, from the second marriage— which finished in divorce when she was twenty.

"Back then," she explains, "in Tennessee you got married to the guy you slept with. But I wouldn't change a thing, because I had both my kids."

Her first attempts at launching a singing career came in the mid-seventies in Nashville, when she would perform in local bars, singing her own compositions. To avoid comparisons with her famous relatives, she would bill herself as "Calhoun Cartier." To complete the ruse, she claimed to be a stripper from Los Angeles.

In 1976 Emmylou Harris covered Carlene's song, "Easy from Now On." Her songwriting seemed to have a life of its own for a while. The Doobie Brothers recorded her "One Step Closer," and The Go-Go's immortalized "I'm The Only One."

She moved to England in 1978, and quickly landed her first record deal. Her debut album, *Carlene Carter* (1978) was produced by British rocker Dave Edmunds. It was there that she met and fell in love with one of Edmunds's best friends, fellow Rockpile rocker Nick Lowe. They were together for six years, and then, as Carter explains it, the marriage "just ran its course."

From the late seventies to the early eighties she released five albums, including the cult-classic disk *Musical Shapes* (1980). Her other albums included *Two Sides to Every Woman* (1979), the r&b flavored *Blue Nun* (1981), and the more techno-pop *C'est C Bon* [sic] (1983). She also starred in the London stage version of the revue/play *Pump Boys and The Dinettes,* with Kiki Dee. Carlene played the role of Purdie, whom she describes as "the lightheaded one" of the two female lead roles.

What was most impressive about Carlene's first turn at a recording career, was her incredible "who's who" list of rock & roll heavies. They include such a diverse roster as Clarence Clemons, Paul Schaffer, Graham Parker & The Rumor, and Paul Carrack (Mike & The Mechanics).

"I used to be wild as far as hanging out, partying a lot. Back in the early eighties and late seventies, when I lived in England it was fashionable to drink in a big way, and I guzzled a lot of champagne," she recalls.

On a promotional concert tour of the United States, Carter performed at the Greenwich Village rock club The Bottom Line. She didn't know it at the time, but her mother June and stepfather Johnny were in the audience that night. Introducing her tongue-in-cheek song about suburban wife-swapping, "Swap-Meat Rag," she announced "If this song doesn't put the 'cu*t' back in 'country,' I don't know what will!" When the press—including *Rolling Stone*—got ahold of that story, she was branded as quite the hellion. "The one time I say something nasty onstage," she recalls, "all the press are there, my parents are there. I didn't make a habit of that, but I became notorious for being that way and I wasn't that way! It just happened on one night that I was joking around with my band. I didn't know who was in the crowd and the whole thing got blown out of proportion. So, because of that I got a label for being a rebel, and I'm not a rebel in any other sense, except I can't be made to be something I'm not."

Of her partying reputation Carter admits, "We were running pretty fast. We'd celebrate during the gigs, and in the dressing rooms before the gigs."

Meanwhile, Carlene's mother, June, and her two aunts, Helen and Anita, had continued to perform as The Carter Family. They carried on the Carter family tradition after matriarch "Mother" Maybelle died in 1978. When the three sisters came to London to perform in 1986, one night her Aunt Anita became ill and couldn't perform. Pulled into the act as an emergency stand-in, Carlene performed that night with her mother and Aunt Helen as the third Carter Family member.

According to June, Carlene was a natural in the act: "She began to feel whatever it is that you're born with that makes you a singing Carter and makes you love and sing that Appalachian mountain harmony. She'd found her way back to traditional country."

"Working with The Carter Family," explains Carlene, "really got me back into country. I loved singing with them, and I loved playing that music. It touched me in a way that nothing I'd done before did. I knew then that I wanted to carry that on in some way, even though it might not be exactly like them. I'm very proud of my heritage, and I felt like I'd been letting them down."

In the late eighties Carlene decided to move back to Nashville, and pull the plug on her solo recording career which—despite fabulous critical reviews—just never seemed to catch fire. "I didn't fit into country *or* rock. I was sick of straddling," she recalls. "It hurt me that Nashville wouldn't accept me for what I was, and I wasn't dumb enough to go ahead and make a sixth album."

Of album number five, Carter lamented, "My last album didn't do nothin'. It was totally not me. Synthesizer pop, everything I hated. So I got discouraged and quit. I decided to take a rest, a long, very long rest."

What she did instead of focusing on her solo recording career was to continue to tour with The Carter Family as a quartet for the next two years. To further entrench herself in rediscovering her roots, she moved into her grandmother Maybelle's old Nashville area house. "I just couldn't let the place where [her sister] Rosie and I grew up become some sort of condo."

As the 1980s were coming to a close, it was suddenly time to return her focus to her solo career. One of the major changes she made in her life was to curb her drinking habit. Looking back at the last decade with a newfound clarity, she claims, "When I think about some of the things I did in the old days, it scares me to death. I'd never trade it for nothing, but I'd never go on stage drunk now. In fact, I don't even drink, period. And I was so reckless, not caring what I said. But I take my career very seriously now. It's what I love most of all, the writing and the performing and making records. To think how close I came to blowing that completely and not getting a second chance . . . well, a lot of people never get to make a comeback, especially to someplace they never got to the first time!"

After Carlene teamed up with current boyfriend Howie Epstein, they began working on the demos for what was to become her big comeback album, *I Fell in Love*. According to her, "I wanted to give country the edge it didn't have. I was so ahead of my time I was doomed. If I had been any more ahead I'd have been too old to do it again!"

Well, fortunately for Carlene, Nashville had suddenly changed. From 1985 to 1989 such genre-broadening women as K. T. Oslin, k. d. lang, and Mary-Chapin Carpenter had brought intelligent lyrics, new themes, new sounds and new energy to country music. Fortunately for Carter, her time up at bat had finally arrived.

When her *I Fell in Love* album was released, *Stereo Review* magazine called it "stunning . . . walking the delicate line between the backwoods strains of her pedigree and a smart beat of contemporary country and neo-rockabilly." In 1992 *Time* magazine referred to her as a "roots rebel," and explained that "*I Fell in Love* was her breakthrough hit—Sylvia Plath at the honky tonk."

The single "I Fell in Love" raced up the charts into the country Top Ten, and the following year she racked up a Grammy nomination for the album of the same name, and an Academy of Country Music nomination for Best New Female Vocalist.

Carlene was elated at finally attaining the success she had sought for so long. "There was a period where I was a little scared that I'd blown my chance. But I think everything that I did, every step I took, every wrong turn led to this. I've matured as a writer and human being. I've got some wisdom under my belt," she said at the time.

"I am in the mode right now where I think country music needs a breath of good-naturedness and a girl who can go out there and have fun," she claims. "Other girls want to do that, but they're afraid they'll seem improper. Why can't you dance and have fun and wear short skirts? I think I *do* have an image of being a little fluffy in some sense, but if people listen to the record [the *I Fell in Love* album], they'll know there's a lot more to me than that—that I can turn right around and write a real serious song like 'Me and the Wildwood Rose.'"

In the song "Me and the Wildwood Rose,"

Carlene is referring to the nickname that her mother gave to her sister Rosie. Amid the song, Carter sings about riding around in her Grandma Maybelle's big Cadillac, and listening to her singing to the girls. The song was such a critical hit that there is even interest from movie producers to expand the vignette-like song into a movie.

One of the keys to the success of the album *I Fell in Love,* was the stellar lineup of guest stars on the album, including guitarists Albert Lee and James Burton, plus vocalists Dave Edmunds, Levon Helm (The Band), Keith Knudsen (The Doobie Brothers), Nicolette Larson, and Kiki Dee.

When it came time to record a follow-up to *I Fell in Love,* Carlene again collaborated with boyfriend Howie Epstein. The results, the rousing, sharp, and exciting *Little Love Letters,* was again a huge smash. The album's first single, "Every Little Thing," sailed up the charts into the country Top Ten, and again threw the spotlight on Carter's role as one of the freshest singers in the nineties music scene. Opening with the unconventional sound of the title cut, the instruments played on the song include the sound of a wheezing liquid dishwasher-soap bottle. Highlights include the beautiful ballad "Unbreakable Heart" (written by Benmont Tench of The Heartbreakers), the declarative "I Love You 'Cause I Want To," the revival meeting-esque "Hallelujah in My Heart," and the sensitive "The Rain"—which Carlene wrote with Elton John's writing partner Bernie Taupin.

When it was released, *Country Music* magazine proclaimed it "a major step forward for Carter into the first rank of country singers." The album was a fulfillment of the great wealth of musical talent that Carlene's *I Fell in Love* showed the promise of, and took it one step further.

Of her collaborative work with Epstein, Carter claims, "If Howie had complete control over what I write, it would come out even more hillbilly. People would think it's just the opposite—that he would be the one who would want to keep it more contemporary, more rock-sounding. The problem is, I just haven't written that many hillbilly songs!"

At long last she is able to say, "I see now that there's a little niche for me. It's a youthful approach for me. I've lived a lot, and I relate to those women who live in a trailer park in Kansas, because I've lived in a trailer, too. Most women who buy records are looking for a little bit of hope. They want someone to tell them it's gonna be okay. I feel like I'm a woman's woman, and I'm always for the girl. And I hope they feel that way about me. Most of all, I want them to know that there's a light at the end of the tunnel."

Thanks to her pair of 1990s hit albums, there's more than just light at the end of the tunnel. For

Carlene Carter, the end of the tunnel has finally led her to artistic success, personal happiness, respect within both the rock and country music realms, and a continuation of the Carter family musical legacy.

Says Carlene, "I want to have fun. Music is fun, I mean, life is hard enough as it is. God created music to heal our souls a bit. If I can be the person who can make someone laugh or giggle or want to shake their butt, then, you know, I want to be that girl." If fun and excitement is what you're looking for in country music — then Carlene Carter definitely *is* that girl!

Chapter Eleven
Suzy Bogguss

Country music has many sides to it. It can be lamenting like the blues, it can be as twangy as a barn dance, or it can be as clear and fresh as a folk song. Suzy Bogguss is from the folky side of the tracks. She doesn't sing songs by Loretta Lynn, she sings songs by Kim Carnes. While she cowgirled herself silly on her 1989 *Somewhere Between* album—her latest and biggest successes have come with her albums *Aces, Voices,* and *Somethin' up My Sleeve,* which sound like they would be just as appropriate wafting out of a Greenwich Village folk club as they would emanating from a country western bar in Nashville.

If Linda Ronstadt; Judy Collins, or Peter, Paul & Mary's Mary Travers were singing country, they'd probably fit right in on one of Suzy Bogguss's nineties albums. Suzy has already been produced by Ronstadt protégé Wendy Waldman, has put Collins's 1969 hit "Someday Soon" in the country Top Ten, and her "Outbound Plane" blends country and folk the same way as Travers's 1973 recording of "Southbound Train." Suzy's music comes more out of this folk tradition, than it does from country. Her musical image is more Colorado than it is Nashville.

When she was a student at Illinois State University, her two passions became music, and jewelry design. When she saw a silver bracelet on one of her dorm mates, she realized that she was capable of designing and making her own version. "I thought, I could make those! What fun!" she claims. She enrolled in a metalsmithing class, and eventually designed and created all kinds of rings, bracelets, necklaces and stickpins. Says Suzy, "I started making bracelets to give as gifts because they were so inexpensive. I'd twist them out of silver wire, solder one end, and that was it."

After she received her B.A. as an art major, she set out into the world to pursue her other love: music. She traveled throughout the United States, Canada and Mexico, singing a blend of country, folk, rock and pop songs. She built her strongest audiences in the Rocky Mountain states of Colorado, Wyoming and Montana. She also developed a following in Chicago and Minneapolis. Her strategy was "to get that eclectic circle going for myself."

Finally, in 1985 she headed for Nashville, and began to focus on a career in country music. The first job she landed found her singing in a rib joint. Eventually she was hired for studio work — recording songwriters' demos.

Like many of the women in this book, Suzy Bogguss too, has a "Dolly Parton connection." In 1986, Suzy was working as one of the amusement park singers at Dollywood in Pigeon Forge, Tennessee, when she was discovered by Liberty Records and signed to a recording deal.

Describing her early musical influences, Boggus explains, "When I was little I started listening to the music my folks listened to, mostly Eddy Arnold's records. His songs were perfect. Then when I grew up, I started listening to artists like Linda Ronstadt, James Taylor, Elton John, Carole King — they were performers who really inspired me. I was influenced by country when I started playing the clubs. I would sing songs by Emmylou Harris and Crosby, Stills and Nash."

Her first two albums, *Moment of Truth* and *Somewhere Between* were decidedly more straight-ahead country/western. On the Wendy Waldman-produced *Somewhere Between* album, the songs Suzy chose to sing had a definite cowboy twang to them. She covered Hank Williams Sr.'s "My Sweet Love Ain't Around," and Merle Haggard's title cut. However the most riotous and raucous song was Bogguss's rousing version of Patsy Montana's 1935 hit "I Want to Be a Cowboy's Sweetheart" — complete with the midsong yodeling. The funny thing is that "I Want to Be a Cowboy's Sweetheart" became the album's most memorable highlight.

In much the same way that Bonnie Raitt became friends with 1930s blues artist Sippie Wallace after covering Wallace's "You Got To Know How," Suzy has become very close to country/western veteran Patsy Montana. Says Bogguss, "She sold a million records—clear back just out of the depression time, and really put country music on the map."

According to Patsy: "I've adopted Suzy Bogguss—for two or three reasons. First reason, she rejuvenated 'Cowboy's Sweetheart,' and she does a great job—she really yodels! And she's got a good voice, what can stop her? I've got an adopted daughter now—I think she's great!"

Not only did she end up with a friend in Patsy Montana, but she also ended up with a husband, from the same album! She covered a song by studio engineer and songwriter Doug Crider called "Hopeless Romantic," and ended up falling in love with him. When they married in 1988— you guessed it—Suzy designed and made the wedding bands. She wanted to add some sense of tradition to the rings, so she made them by melting down and recasting heirlooms from members of both of their families.

To this day she still loves to work in precious metals. One of the pieces she designed is an elaborate earring which is available through her fan club. According to Suzy, "There's something really challenging about metal, because it's so difficult to work with. You have to have a strategy. It's not like a painting where you can just cover up your mistakes and go on. I get a lot of creative thinking done when I'm working with metal. I might be sitting there working on something for three hours, and no one can see the progress but me. In the back of my mind, though, I'm thinking, 'Wow! I just got an idea for a song!' "

When Suzy's *Somewhere Between* album was released, *Stereo Review* magazine glowed, "It heralds the arrival both of a serious new country talent and of a producer finally coming into her own . . . Dollywood's loss, it happily appears, is everyone else's gain." Her 1990 album release, *Moment of Truth,* produced by Jimmy Bowen and Suzy, continued the promise of her debut disk.

While she was still building an audience, Suzy went into the studio, and began working on her third album, *Aces,* which would become known as her big breakthrough album. Again, she co-produced it with Jimmy Bowen. The outcome was a sheer smash, and it became Bogguss's first "Gold" album, and yielded three Top Ten hits: "Someday Soon," "Outbound Plane," and "Letting Go."

According to her, that album represented a

turning point for her. "With *Aces,*" she explains, "I felt like I'd grown up as an artist. Up until that time, I kept analyzing every song I sang. I started out in this business by playing small concerts in coffee houses and truck stops. I had to be very versatile and it really prepared me to just get out there and sing songs I really wanted to do. I was lucky my co-producer on the album, Jimmy Bowen, gave me the freedom to do what I wanted to do with my songs."

The album *Aces* is sheer perfection. From Nancy Griffith's "Outbound Plane" to Kim Carnes's and Wendy Waldman's "Still Hold On," Suzy Bogguss walks the line between folk/rock and country, and creates her own unique niche throughout. Her lilting pop/country/folk delivery shines on every song.

Suzy began winning hearts and awards right from the start. In 1988 she won an Academy of Country Music Award as the most promising newcomer of the year. In 1992 Suzy won the Horizon Award from the Country Music Association, as the singer most likely to have the brightest career future. "I was very surprised," says Suzy of the Horizon Award. "I never thought I'd actually win. I mean, I've been going to the CMA Award shows for years. It didn't actually hit me that there was a chance I could win, so I didn't even prepare a speech. I was talking to Mary-Chapin Carpenter after the show. She won for Best Female Vocalist, and we were both saying we couldn't believe it. Mary-Chapin and I have a lot in common. She's a singer/ songwriter who started playing in coffee houses, and so did I."

What Suzy remembers the most about the awards show that night, is that it was a real comedy of errors. According to her, "During the show, I had a terrible trauma. I was sitting in the audience, and I had left word with several people backstage to make sure I had plenty of time to change into my costume for the performance. I was wearing a long dress, and I knew I wouldn't be comfortable singing 'Outbound Plane' in that. Pam Tillis and Billy Dean were performing in the same segment with me, so I really started to get nervous when I noticed they were leaving to go backstage. I looked at my husband, Doug, and he said, 'Well, you told two people, so they'll come get you.' The next thing I knew, the show went to a commercial break, and the announcer says, 'And coming up after this—the Horizon Award.' I absolutely freaked out! Of course, I ran backstage with maybe three minutes to change when I actually needed twenty."

"I got to the dressing room and changed as quickly as I could," she continues. "The stage crew was calling me to get to the backstage area. I ran up there, but I still had to put my boots on. Then I realized I didn't have my belt, so I'm yelling like crazy at my road manager to go back to the dressing room for me. While Pam Tillis was singing, there was complete mayhem backstage. Billy Dean and the guys who were standing around were laughing hysterically watching me try to lace up my boots. But, I guess winning the award made having to go through all that, worth it!"

While her 1992 hit, "Letting Go," was still climbing up the charts, her next album was ready for October release. So, instead of killing the momentum of the single by releasing a new album without the song on it, Liberty Records decided to add it to the new disk. Explains Suzy, "The decision by the record company to include this on two albums had to do with the release date of *Voices in the Wind*. They decided they were going to release the new album before Christmas, and in order to get it in the stores, they would have to go ahead with it in October. 'Letting Go' was still going to be out, so the record label decided that rather than shortening the life of the single because of the new album, they would rather put it on the new album as well. It sort of helped bridge the gap. It's a very unique thing to do, because it actually means less money to the record company and a bonus track for whoever buys the record."

Explaining her choice of material for the *Voices in the Wind* album, Bogguss proclaims, "I love ballads, especially the sad ones. Although,

I'm noticing some of them are a little hard to get through in concert. Cheryl Wheeler's song, 'Don't Wanna,' touches me every time I sing it because I've experienced lost love. That song is a heartstopper. My baby is 'In the Day.' I wrote it and produced it. I think 'Eat at Joe's' is a lot of fun. I've had a great time doing that one on stage. I dress like a waitress—complete with apron."

When the album was released, *The New York Times* wrote, "Bogguss's music reflects the winds of change at work on country's traditional male-female roles." *Country Music* magazine proclaimed, "Suzy Bogguss is simply the best of the new crop of women vocalists."

"I titled this album *Voices in the Wind* because I felt so connected to each one of these people in these songs—their feelings, their tragedy, their trials in life or excitements," says Suzy. "You illuminate parts of life for just a second so that people reflect—so that someone goes, 'Oh yeah, I forgot about that.' 'I've been a real creep to my husband this week,' or 'I forgot how much I loved my grandma. I haven't thought about that for a little while.'"

Suzy proved herself a girl for all seasons in the winter of 1993-1994. Her fifth album, *Something Up My Sleeve* crystalized the groundwork she had laid with her previous releases. She had two simultaneous hits on the charts with the songs "Just Like The Weather" and "Hey Cinderella."

The LP is the most consistently pleasing of her career. She was also at the top of the charts with her version of "Take It To The Limit" on the Number One "Double Platinum" album *Common Thread: Songs Of The Eagles,* effectively taking the self-produced songs to the "max." When Asleep At The Wheel released their album *Tribute To The Music Of Bob Wills & The Texas Playboys,* Suzy yodeled and country swinged her way into "Old Fashioned Love" as a duet with Asleep's leader, Ray Benson.

Just as her recording career took off, her designing career heated up as well. Suzy struck a business deal with a clothing manufacturer in San Francisco called Baguda Wear, and turned out a line of leather jackets that were carried by Nordstroms department stores on the West Coast. It was marketed as "The Suzy Bogguss Leather Collection." "The people who presented this idea to me did so in a very open manner," she explains. "This is really like a heyday for me. I've had a bit to do with the designs that have come along for me in the past, so this was like getting to close my eyes and picture what I consider the perfect outfit and then have someone make it for me for free!"

Of the designing end of the task, she claims, "It's been cool for me because it's like when you go to a store and say, 'Now if this coat only had that collar, I'd buy it.' Now I can put together all the different pieces I like."

"Some of the jackets have a Western flair to them," says Suzy. "Most of them are made out of lamb suede or lamb leather. Some of them also have the Chimayo Indian weaving in them. It's this special kind of weave done by a particular tribe out in New Mexico. I've met some of the people out there, and they're also helping to design the buttons."

Does this mean that she is planning to leave country music for her designing career? Hardly. "No, never!" she exclaims, "I can't imagine my life without music." Thank goodness, because her fans eagerly await more chapters in the country/folk saga of this exciting creative work-in-progress known as Suzy Bogguss.

Chapter Twelve
Shelby Lynne

With a sleek new look, and a hot new Texas swing album, Shelby Lynne is suddenly the hottest new country girl to watch for. One listen to her brilliant *Temptation* album, and you'll find yourself instantly hooked. Shelby, who also switched record labels and producers for this new disk, has finally been matched with music and arrangements that are as exciting and powerful as her 10,000 watt voice.

What a dramatic difference, direction can mean! On Lynne's 1991 album, *Soft Talk,* she was photographed on the cover in a soft focus, making her look like a sophisticated quiet and mellow country balladeer. The music on the album finds Lynne struggling to lower her gutsy, powerful vocal capacity. The album isn't bad per se, but it underplayed the singer's vast talent.

Abracadabra! From out of left field came Shelby's 1993 album, *Temptation,* with a new look, new sound, new photographer, new manager, new label, new excitement. With her hair dyed copper red and cropped little-boy short, a black beret on her head, and a 1930s style black dress with a plunging neckline, Lynne looked like Bonnie — of the bank robbing duo Bonnie & Clyde. The image is startling, striking, and suggests just enough of a degree of "naughty" to make the gamine-appearing Lynne look enticingly seductive.

And the music is pure country swing that seems a divinely inspired stylistic mix of Bob Willis, The Andrews Sisters, Peggy Lee, and Asleep at the Wheel. Produced by Brent Maher, who worked magic with The Judds, this one album fulfills the promise that her first three albums only hinted at.

Shelby Lynne's road to fame in the country-music arena has not always been a smooth one. When she sings of pain or heartbreak she knows of both commodities firsthand. And, when she sings with unwavering strength and determination, it is because she has had to draw upon both resources in the past.

Born Shelby Lynn Moorer, October 22, 1968 in Quantico, Virginia, her family eventually moved to the Mobile, Alabama vicinity. That is where Shelby, and her younger sister Allison grew up with their parents Vernon and Laura. Tragically, Vernon, an ex-marine with a drinking problem, was abusive towards her mother, Laura. This was a terrible secret that Shelby and Allison had to grow up with.

Says Shelby, "In high school, I was a loner. I had friends, but not any close ones. I didn't *want* any close friends. I didn't want to be around anybody. I didn't *like* anybody. I was kind of a hood, kind of tough, a didn't-take-any-crap kind of thing. I didn't study. I made poor grades. I didn't want to be in school. I was wrapped up in my music—that was pretty much all I felt like was really mine. I was very mature for my age. I had to grow up real fast. I was not interested in high-school kids. I was an adult when I was in high school."

Her being a loner can be directly attributed to her home life. When her father began to become abusive toward her and her sister, they moved out with their mother.

It was a summer evening in 1986 when "the accident"—as Shelby refers to it—occurred. Shelby was seventeen at the time, and Allison was fourteen. Their father showed up at the house in the middle of the night, and their mother ran outside to see what the commotion was about. Regardless of whatever dialogue transpired, Vernon aimed a gun at Laura, shot and killed her, and then shot and killed himself.

Shelby was awakened from a sound sleep by the sounds of gunfire. She went out into the yard only to discover both of her parents dead there. To this day, she still has trouble speaking about "the accident."

"I can't talk about it," she says. "It's over. It doesn't have anything to do with anything. I'm in this career because I'm talented and I have something to share with people. It doesn't have anything to do with my mother and dad being deceased. It happened, and it's real frustrating for me. But I'd rather not discuss it."

Shelby and Allison moved in with relatives, and tried to put the memory of "the accident" behind them. Immediately after graduating from high school, Shelby got married. However, it lasted just over a year. "I was a baby when I got married," she explains. "It was like a trip out of town. We're good friends now. But I'm always looking! I think I was too young to know anything about it at the time."

Although still a teenager, Shelby had already begun going to local talent contests, and blowing people away with her singing. She dropped her last name, took her middle name and added an extra "e" to it, and left for Nashville with a new identity. She was ready for a bright new future.

"Nobody could pronounce Moorer," she confesses. As for the "e," she explains, "I put it there myself because I didn't want to be confused with Loretta Lynn."

She tried out for a singing role that was being cast at Opryland USA. Although she didn't land the part, her powerful voice caught the attention of a songwriter who was present at the audition that day. He invited Shelby to start recording song demos for him, and she agreed. When someone from the TV show "Nashville Now" heard one of the demo tapes Shelby had sung on, within two weeks of having recorded the song, she found herself booked on the show. Based on her performance on the TV program, she snagged a recording contract of her own at Epic Records.

During her time with Epic, Shelby released three albums: *Sunrise* in 1989, *Tough All Over* in 1990, and *Soft Talk* in 1991. However, it was not until the new album, *Temptation,* that Shelby really broke through. "I love those albums," she says of the three Epic disks, "They are very much a part of me. So much of what I brought to *Temptation* I learned while recording my earlier albums."

Her first Top 40 hit came with the song "The Hurtin' Side," from her debut album. Also on that album is her fantastically searing version of the 1948 song "I Love You So Much It Hurts." The *Tough All Over* album produced three hits for Shelby: "Things Are Tough All Over," "I'll Lie Myself to Sleep," and "What About the Love We Made." In 1991, at the age of twenty-two, The Academy of Country Music named her the year's Best New Female Artist. The press, likewise loved her. *USA Today* proclaimed, "Shelby Lynne breaks through the country pack. This girl can sing the chrome off a trailer hitch." And, *The Tennessean* raved, "Voices like this come along once a generation. With her flame-thrower delivery, you know you're listening to someone special."

Although those first three albums gave her a great start, several reviewers were quick to note that she had yet to have an album that accurately captured the power and strength of her in-concert and in-person voice. Said Lynne of her association with Epic Records, "They don't know what to do with me. I am totally what they hate, because I'm not an easy package to market: I look like a twelve-year-old boy and sound like a forty-five-year-old torch singer. They must have a terrible time with me. Meanwhile, I just concentrate on my music. I'm not doing this to make quick number-one records. I tell radio people all the time I don't give a damn if they play my records or not! The public will ultimately demand what they want to hear."

Shelby almost immediately began winning hearts within the Nashville community. When George Jones recorded a recent all-duet album, Lynne recorded the song "If I Could Bottle This Up," with him. Jones was so impressed with her, he refers to her as "my little adopted daughter." She also has a special affection for Tammy Wynette, and recorded her own version of Tammy's "Alive And Well." Wynette returned the compliment by declaring Lynne's "the best voice in country music." Tammy further claims, "There are girls who sing, and girls who sing with soul—Shelby Lynne sings with a *lot* of soul!" And, Randy Travis has referred to her as "incredible."

Shelby also landed a part in the Willie Nelson and Kris Kristofferson made-for-TV movie, "Another Pair Of Aces." "It was hardly an acting role," she laughs. "I played myself. I didn't even have any dialogue. Willie's a crook gone good, Kris is the sheriff, and I'm a saloon singer. I sang two songs. One, they played while Kris was makin' love to this woman. So, so much for my big acting career!" She needn't worry, because there are several big things to come in her future.

To promote her first three albums, Shelby toured around the countryside. Although she admits that riding around on a bus for hours on end, "gets old," she enthusiastically says, "But, I still love being out on tour, doing what I love. The towns and the auditoriums are all the same to me. They all run together. All I ever see is the backside of an auditorium. I'm not into seeing the sights. I'm just there to sing. That's the highlight of my day. A live performance is the payoff for me. I get to meet the people, and I get to share with them what I do best. That's my job. That's what I love."

Although she only stands 5 feet, 1 inch tall, Shelby is quite a strong and determined young lady. "I have a real hard time doing photo sessions. I'm not a Barbie — I'm a musician," she claims. "It's not natural for me to be in front of the camera and be voluptuous and gorgeous. It's not my thing to do. I'm insecure because I'm very inexperienced, and I never feel comfortable enough to let loose and make a real relaxed, friendly kind of picture. Photographers always say such things as 'Okay, smile. Show me some teeth.' And I'm like, 'I'll bust your mouth.

Leave me alone.' I'm not out to impress anybody. I'm very honest and open about my feelings, if you ask me. *Only* if you ask me."

She also admits that she struggles with her own temper sometimes. Says Shelby, "I'm the first to admit it. I will break furniture. It's not something I'm proud of. I'm working on it, though. It's part of growing up. When people aren't on the same wave length with me, I have no patience. I tend to blow up sometimes."

Making the shift from Epic Records to Mercury Records' Morgan Creek label in 1993 signaled all kinds of changes for Shelby. From her short-cropped haircut on the cover, to the thrilling and stirring country swing sound on the album, there are signs of the emergence of a new Shelby Lynne. She looks and sounds more confident than ever before.

When the album was released, *USA Today* glowed that, "This amazing young singer (she's twenty-four) seems finally to have found her musical stride . . . It's a gotta-hear kind of thing."

According to her, "We went for more of an Irving Berlin lyric with a Bob Wills beat. And you know what Bob Wills said: 'It ain't music if you can't dance to it!' " Well, Shelby certainly has Nashville dancing to a new tune with her *Temptation* album. From the exciting title cut, to the swinging "Some of That True Love," to the hit "Feelin' Kind of Lonely Tonight," Shelby is right on target at last.

"I have always felt the need to sing," she claims. "I never considered doing anything else." Thank goodness Shelby Lynne is here to stay, because hers is one of the unique and special voices in country music today!

Chapter Thirteen
k. d. lang

A "chameleon"—that's the best way to describe k.
d. lang. When she wanted to blend rock with country swing—she did it on her *Angel with a Lariat* album. When she wanted to mirror Patsy Cline—she
took it to the nth degree by teaming with Cline's producer Owen Bradley. And, when she decided that
she'd rather emulate non-country sixties chanteuses
like Julie London and Peggy Lee—she went all the
way, and grabbed another Grammy to boot!

The unique Ms. lang is someone who makes you
ask questions. "Has k.d. turned her back on country?" "Has Nashville written her off?" These are
burning questions in the country-music world. Well,
I've got a better one: "What's the difference?" Did
anyone squawk when Patsy recorded middle-of-the-
road pop like "Bill Bailey, Won't You Please Come
Home," or Irving Berlin's "Always?" With the success of k.d.'s "Platinum" lounge-singer deluxe album, *Ingenue,* she merely proves that one musical

genre isn't enough to hold her. Didn't we all know that already?

As a performer, lang is hard to ignore. How could you miss her? It's like going to Paris and missing the Eiffel Tower! k.d. has always dressed, behaved, posed, positioned, postured, and poised herself to be noticed. The tailored clothes, the mannish haircut, the insistence that all of the letters in her name be spelled in lower case symbols are all part of the plan.

After she covered Patsy's lesser-known hit "Three Cigarettes in an Ashtray," k.d. was immediately dubbed the cross-dressing successor to the Cline throne. When she expanded her musical horizons to encompass the stylings of Doris Day on "Ingenue," did she lose fans? No—she gained them. When mannish lang announced that she was gay—only people living under rocks should have registered surprise. So, what's the beef? (Speaking of beef—well, more about that later.)

k. d. lang has become one of the most expressive singers in late eighties/early nineties country. She has brought another focus to it—and, like K. T. Oslin—she has drawn a new audience to the country-music section of the local record shops.

Although she has shifted gears, she hasn't necessarily changed. It's just that the music swirling around her has less of the signature country twang than her first three albums. As a country artist, k.d. was selling her way into "Platinum" certifications before Reba McEntire logged a million-seller. With three Grammy Awards to her credit, k. d. lang forced the record industry to look upon country music as something more than big hairdo ladies, and songs about truckers.

She was born Kathy Dawn Lang in the small town of Consort, Alberta, Canada—population 714. "We were a pretty normal family," recalls lang. "We had supper every night at six o'clock, and Saturday mornings I had to vacuum the carpet and clean the bathrooms."

Living out in the rural expanses of Alberta, growing up there were lots of outdoorsy fun things to do. "My father treated me like a tomboy," explains lang. "I did very 'boy' things with him. He bought me a motorcycle when I was nine; I've been riding cycles for twenty-two years. I was a marksman; I used to shoot guns with him—revolvers, shotguns. But we shot targets; I never killed animals . . . I remember him getting me an electric guitar for Christmas when I was in grade six."

When k.d. was twelve years old, her father suddenly got up one day, and left the family—forever. "I loved both my parents very, very much, and of course I went into shock when my father left," she confesses. "It was sudden and drastic. I didn't hear from him for about eight years, until I ran into him on the street in Edmonton one time. I haven't really talked to him since. I think I'm just processing it now."

According to her, the element of surprise is what got to her the most: "I knew there were troubles, but him leaving the way he did was a shock, and very hard for me to watch my mother go through. He left everything, so my mother would teach in the day and then go down and try to run the store. I had to take on some of the responsibilities, whether it was working in the drugstore or getting home on time so my mother wouldn't worry. I went from being a kid to being an adult very fast."

From the very beginning, k.d. has always indulged herself in her eccentricities. At the age of five she got hooked on performing after a local tap-dancing recital she appeared in. Her "look-at-me" clothing style dates back to a pair of leather bell-bottoms she had in the sixth grade.

After high-school graduation, she studied art at Red Deer College in Alberta. She also joined a group of performance artists whose most famous routine was the reenactment of a heart transplant operation.

In 1982 k.d. was cast in a play emulating the life of Patsy Cline. The introduction to Cline and her music made a lasting impression on her. "Something clicked between Patsy and me," she claims. "It enabled me to do country with a sense of humor but also with a great deal of emotion and respect."

Her singing career started slowly and tentatively, but it quickly picked up steam. Billed as "Kathy Lang" on the live Canadian TV variety show "Sun Country," she made her broadcast debut. Her mode of attire in those days consisted of full-skirted cowgirl dresses, and fifties rhinestone cat's-eye glasses. She looked like Pee Wee Herman, in drag. In addition, she used to love to pin little plastic farm animals, and little plastic corral fences on her cowgirl shirts. On the show she sang a song she had written called "Friday Dance Promenade," and was heralded on the air as "the Alberta Rose, the pride of the West." Little did they know, but the Alberta Rose had yet to fully blossom.

Inspired by poet e. e. cummings, that same year she decided to start spelling her name in all lowercase letters. However, the "pièce de résistance" came when she shaved her head—right before a concert. "I started to feel this weird change in my personality," she remembers. "I was getting vain and very concerned about the way I looked. Then I needed to give myself a haircut, and for some reason I just kept cutting and cutting and cutting. When I finally looked into the mirror, I was bald. I had to perform that night in front of 3,500 people, which was huge for me [at the time]. So, I wore a hat, but then in the middle of the show, I took the hat off. I heard 3,500 people gasp. And then I just went, 'Yeah,' because it gave me this incredible [rush], this incredible feeling of breaking through."

In 1985, k.d. was exported to Asia, to appear as one of the musical acts representing Canada at the Expo In Japan. It was there that k.d. met Ben Mink, who was the member of another Canadian group. He joined the band she had put together, The Reclines, and since that time they have been music-writing partners.

She was first spotted by Carl Scott, an artists' relations vice-president for Warner Brothers Records. At the time she was performing in her swirling cowgirl dresses, which she had also begun to sew plastic toy farm animals to. Her stage set that night with the Edmonton Symphony consisted of bales of hay and stand-up cut-outs of red barns.

Scott recalls, "She was totally superior to anyone I had ever heard. She was very shy and withdrawn back then, but on stage she was completely in charge. When she gets out on a stage, she's queen of her domain. She understands everything about it, and she loves it."

When Seymour Stein, president of Warner-distributed Sire Records, saw her, he flipped. It was Stein who signed Madonna in 1982, so he knew talent when he saw it. "I was just transfixed," says Stein of his first sight of lang. "She was wearing country square-dance clothes and real short hair, but you could close your eyes and imagine her singing anything — show tunes, R&B, hits from the fifties, country classics."

Recorded in London, England, in the first half of 1986, and released the following year, her first album, *Angel with a Lariat,* signaled a star in the making. The album itself featured an odd assortment of hybrid tunes — from the bizarre squaredance calls of "Turn Me Round," to the comic "Watch Your Step Polka," to Ben Mink's rockabilly "Tune into My Wave," to a campy and pepped-up remake of Lynn Anderson's syrupy "Rose Garden." Listening to it is like attending a barn dance on Mars.

Produced by arty rocker Dave Edmunds, the tone of the album is a tongue-in-cheek take-off of corn-ball country. On too many cuts, k.d.'s subtle artistry seems buried under the music. The entire album seems played for camp—up until the last cut, which is the mind-blowing remake of Patsy Cline's "Three Cigarettes in the Ashtray," which is sheer brilliance.

That one song alone paved the way for her first true masterpiece of an album, 1988's *Shadowland,* an unabashed tribute to Patsy, without recording a single Cline classic. Instead, k.d. teamed with Patsy's legendary producer, Owen Bradley. The results had everybody in Nashville saying, "If Patsy were alive, this is an album she would record."

In the meantime she had recorded a duet version of Roy Orbison's "Crying" with Orbison, which became popular. When Orbison filmed his excellent Cinemax TV special, lang—along with Bonnie Raitt and Jennifer Warnes—provided the background vocals. The results can be heard on the excellent 1989 Orbison album, *Black & White Night.*

With the Orbison connection, and the Patsy connection established, k. d. lang was suddenly the media's darling—the new link between pop/rock and country, and a new bridge between traditional country music and the post-punk modern music scene. In 1988 the Orbison/lang version of "Crying" gave lang her first Grammy Award, in the Best Country Collaboration category.

It was Mary Martin of RCA Records who introduced k.d. to producer Owen Bradley. At the time

Bradley had been ill, but came out of retirement when he heard k.d. sing on a videotape Martin gave him. He was so excited that he gladly reentered the recording studio for the first time in ages.

From the first sweeping notes of "Western Skies," it is clear that this expertly crafted album is the perfect embodiment of a singer at the top of her form. The serious artistry that k.d. displays throughout is chilling. Unlike the production on her debut album, on the *Shadowland* LP her voice is creamy and lush as it virtually floats over the crisp arrangements. From the lamenting "Lock, Stock and Teardrops," to the bouncy "Sugar Moon," to the blue classic "Black Coffee," k.d. is sublime.

To complete the Patsy Cline conjuring, vocal group the Jordanaires—who once backed up Patsy, and Cline's best friend Loretta Lynn, make guest appearances on the album. Lynn appears with fellow Nashville legends Kitty Wells and Brenda Lee on the girl-talk quartet arrangement called the "Honky Tonk Angels' Medley."

The *Shadowland* album became an instant country hit. It sold a million copies, and was certified "Platinum." Suddenly, k. d. lang was becoming the hot new voice in country. *Rolling Stone* magazine said of *Shadowland* in their four-star review, "lang sets off explosions on almost every song." Although she sold records like crazy, country radio somehow managed to ignore her completely.

By now her entire image had changed. Gone were the cowgirl outfits and plastic toy farm animals. k.d.

had modified her frills and now dressed like a stylish but androgynous man. She kind of looked like a female Elvis. According to lang, "Androgyny to me is making your sexuality available, through your art, to everyone. Like Elvis, like Mick Jagger, like Annie Lennox or Marlene Dietrich—using the power of both male and female."

The following year, k.d. got back together with Ben Mink, and they began writing country songs that reflected what lang had polished and gleaned from working with Owen Bradley. The outcome was another "Platinum" album, *Absolute Torch and Twang.* Lang and Mink's compositions—including "Luck In My Eyes," "Pullin' Back The Reins," and the autobiographical "Big Boned Gal"—stood up perfectly on the same album with Willie Nelson's "Three Days." All of the songs are unified with crisp production, and k.d. is displaying the fully blossomed confidence that her first album lacked.

When Grammy Award time came around, k.d. grabbed the Best Female Country Vocal honors for *Absolute Torch and Twang.* One would have thought that this honor alone would have convinced Nashville to embrace lang wholeheartedly. However, that was not quite the case. And again, she was ignored by country radio.

If you can say that a million-selling singing star has a cult following, then that is the case. Instead of doing things to endear herself to the country establishment, k.d. used her newfound celebrity to dive into the middle of a huge controversy—involving, of all things—the beef industry.

As a child, k.d. had grown up in the middle of cattle country, and was raised on roast beef. However, she had since become a vegetarian. So, what's the problem? Well, it happened when the antimeat organization People for the Ethical Treatment of Animals (PETA) asked k.d. to star in its first protest commercial. In the ad, k.d. is seen with her arm around Lulu the cow, stating to the camera, "We all love animals, but why do we call some 'pets' and some 'dinner'? If you knew how meat was made, you'd probably lose your lunch. I know—I'm from cattle country, and that's why I'm a vegetarian. Meat stinks, and not just for animals, but for human health and the environment."

Where does meat come from? Oh, middle America cattle country. And what is the most listened to music there? Country music. Oops, major problem, k.d.

Well, when the TV show "Entertainment Tonight" broadcast a piece on it, the story was all over the news. Says lang, "The Canadian Cattle Commission reacted very strongly, which started a whole chain of reactions through the American Cattle Association and the meat industries. [Country] radio stations started banning my records—which is a joke, because the stations that banned my records never played them anyway. Then of course, I was the brunt of a lot of editorials and comic strips."

According to her, "PETA never had to pay the money to run the ads because we got so much controversy going. Also, my record sales went from something like 250 a day to 1,200 a day for three months. That's not why I did it, but that's what controversy can do."

The next topic of controversy came when she publicly spoke of her lesbianism to a reporter for gay magazine *The Advocate*. According to Warner Brothers' Carl Scott, "She called me up and said, 'I think I just "came out" to *The Advocate*.' I said, 'Oh, shit.' But it hasn't hurt at all. People admire her for expressing herself and being who she is and getting rid of the baggage."

According to k.d., "I think it's important for people to come out, because it's broadening the acceptability walls. But I always thought I was 'out.' I presented myself as myself. I didn't try to dispel lesbian rumors. I sang songs like 'Bopalina,' which is about my girlfriend. I didn't take boyfriends to the Grammys. I didn't do anything to cover it up; I just lived my life. There was a part of me that really didn't think it was important to make an announcement. But to the gay community, saying 'I'm a lesbian' is dispelling any doubt."

Having flown fearless into the face of controversy, and having emerged only stronger, it was time for k.d. to explore other sides of herself. Of the influence that she learned she had, lang contemplated, "One of the things it displayed to me, though is that people *are* watching me, and that I am in a position of influence, and that's an interesting thing to realize. I look back on it now, and I just have to say,

'Wow,' because it totally opened the door for me [artistically]. There have always been things like that in my career that aren't contrived or premeditated, but seem to have some sort of profound effect on my direction and my overall approach. I spoke out for PETA because it's a strong belief of mine, but the fact that the whole thing blew up so huge and that it was so ugly was just a real strong indication that it was time for me to move on."

Having gotten the Patsy Cline urgings out of her system, it was time for something completely new. "I think the departure from Patsy Cline's guidance, so to speak, came with the end of *Shadowland*," says lang. "I feel that her influence in my life was actually to bring me to *Shadowland,* but it still wasn't time to move on. I still had *Torch and Twang* inside of me. Then even during that tour, I felt, uh oh, a change is coming!"

The change that came was to be called *Ingenue*. According to her, "Coming to the end of the *Torch and Twang* tour, I felt it was time for me to move on from country. I mean, here I had won the Grammy, but I still wasn't getting any airplay, and even the fact that I had been as creative as possible with country music and I had basically run the course. It's like a lover that you know it is time to leave. The country community treated me well, but they didn't treat me great. I do think that in some way that community will be relieved, 'cause they won't have me to deal with me anymore; I'm talking specifically on the business aspect. I think the fans will come with me actually because I'd like to think it's sort of like Roy Orbison or Ray Charles, the people who can be just singers, you know? You can have country fans and also just be a singer and that actually is what appeals most to me, just being known as a singer and not one specific genre."

Out of love comes pain. Out of pain comes art. That is basically the thematic story behind lang's fourth album, *Ingenue*. It was based on the real-life unrequited love she had for a married woman. Knowing that, the songs "Constant Craving," "Season of Hollow Soul," and "Tears of Love's Recall" take on a new meaning. They are the fruit of loving someone who doesn't love you.

The regret of this love that never had a chance to grow caused k.d. to become cynical about love in general. "Maybe I've developed my spirituality around coping, but I truly believe it's the law of nature that love isn't something we necessarily own. It isn't necessarily shared. There are moments of sharing, but I don't think there are any rules."

With regard to writing each one of the songs, and feeling each one of the songs, lang illuminates, "I think that what's great about this record is that it was a body of work that was conceived and born within ten months. That may give it a special continuity, that it's sort of plucked from an emotional period in my life."

The resulting album is a masterpiece in a totally different genre. Musically, there are enough twanging pedal steel guitars and lilting melodies to tie *Ingenue* to k.d.'s country work. However, unlike her other albums, there aren't any polkas or barn-dance numbers either.

Rolling Stone magazine, in its review of *Ingenue* was at a loss for words when it came time to explain the genre of music it represented. They called it, "a quietly compelling work that suggests the sort of countrypolitan music that Patsy Cline might have sung had she been, well, a Canadian performance artist." That's one way to put it.

What does exist on *Ingenue,* however, is an album of luxurious country tinged mellow music, with deeply introspective lyrics, lush arrangements, and k.d. at her most interpretive. She is in a blue mood, and she wallows in it. "Save Me" sings of love's passion, and the temptations that it conjures. In "The Mind of Love," k.d. holds a dialogue with herself about thinking with her head as opposed to thinking with her heart. Towards the end of the album comes "Outside Myself," in which k.d. sings of having put this love mentally on ice. The album's one lighter number, "Miss Chatelaine," in which lang laughs at her "in love" self, and how — while in love — she becomes her bubbling alterego, Miss Chatelaine.

"It's definitely Doris Day in the fifties going to Paris and feeling very continental and still being very naive at the same time," says lang, explaining the musical and thematic content of the *Ingenue* album. "I think that one of the great things about this record and one of the approaches I'm trying to take is not deliver any specific categories or titles to this type of music but rather to allow the listener and critics to come up with what they feel are my references; because, so far, they have all been right, and my references are so broad and I am proud of them. I don't think that it's a retrospective album. I don't think that it tries to emulate anybody in particular, but there are certain points of reference that you can see."

Ingenue became k.d.'s third consecutive "Platinum" album, and the single "Constant Craving" not only became a hit, but won the Best Female Pop Performance award at the Grammys. Not only did her shift out of hard-core country not lose her any ground, it again proved that the fans she had made in country music were sticking by her.

In the summer of 1993, when k.d. made some disparaging press remarks about being shunned by Nashville, several prominent music executives argued. According to Bill Ivey, director of the Country Music Association, "People in Nashville had a lot of confidence in k.d. Everybody admires her singing, and I think everybody thought she was a breath of fresh air."

"Some people embraced her wholeheartedly, as I did, and thought she was refreshing and wonderful," said Bob Saporiti, vice president of marketing at the Nashville office of Warner Brothers Records. "She was just before the big country boom, and if she had just put out her first album now, there would be no big deal." Another major Nashville k. d. lang supporter is country legend Minnie Pearl.

After all that talk about leaving country, and the hurt and resentment that k.d. felt by not being embraced more openly by Nashville, her next recording project — it turned out — had country elements. It was the soundtrack to the 1993 film *Even Cowgirls Get the Blues*. According to lang collaborator Ben Mink, "We had one day where we did a polka, a jazz-fusion tune, a country waltz, and a Sly & The Family Stone boogie tune." It turned out eclectically perfect for k. d. lang! k.d. was also on hand to sing with another controversial hit-maker. Her duet with Elton John, "Teardrops" open his 1993 *Duets* album and perfectly sets the hit album into gear.

Acting is something that intrigues lang. She made her film debut in the 1991 Canadian movie, *Salmonberries,* by German director Percy Aldon (*Bagdad Cafe*). In the film lang plays an androgynous half-Eskimo girl. She also has spoken several times about wanting to star in a Broadway revival of "Annie Get Your Gun." Sounds like perfect casting: k. d. lang as Annie Oakley!

Whether or not k. d. lang's next album is more of what she calls "post-nuclear cabaret" like *Ingenue,* or if she gets more entrenched in country, or whatever, her original fans are sure to follow. Even if she never does another country album in her career, the impact that she has made on today's country music is still being felt. Her first three albums are strong reasons for the current upsurgence in the "new traditionalist" movement in country music today.

k. d. lang is one of the main reasons why country

music's appeal is so strong now. She attracts an artier crowd than many country stars on the market place. And, when she has their attention, she leaves them constantly craving more.

Chapter Fourteen
Tanya Tucker

As a singing star, Tanya Tucker has had one of the most amazing careers in the music business — country, pop, or any other genre. In terms of the age at which her professional recording career began — she has had one of the longest star-status runs of any of the women who currently shape the face of 1990s country music.

Aside from the fact that Tanya had her first Number One hit, "Delta Dawn" in 1972, when she was just 13 years old, since that time she has virtually lived her very colorful roller-coaster life on the covers of *The National Enquirer, People* magazine, and *The Star.* There have been several times when her legendary boozing and partying, her headline-grabbing affairs, and her single motherhood have eclipsed her singing. Yet, in the last four years, Tucker has revamped her life and her career to achieve her greatest streak of success and commercial popularity. In a business that virtually chews up and spits out new stars annually — Tanya Tucker is a brilliant survivor!

With her 1991 *What Do I Do with Me* album, and 1992's *You Can't Run from Yourself,* Tanya has seen her career transformed from progressively chugging along—into a certified "Gold" winning streak. She hasn't seen such an extended vein of gold since she was a singing teenager back in the seventies.

Known for years as a notorious party animal, Tanya is now the mother of two young children, and her wild instincts have been tempered a bit. This is not to say that she has joined a convent and eschewed the wild life either! Quite the contrary. She is currently Black Velvet Canadian Whiskey's "Black Velvet Lady" in their ad campaigns, and they are the sponsors of her concert tours. The never-married Tanya still makes headlines with her relationships ("Tanya Tucker: I've Got Two Men In My Life—But Neither's Mr. Right" / *The Star* August 31, 1993), but her image is more that of a worldly-wise and sophisticated liberated lady than it is of her early eighties persona as a free-spirited country hellion.

According to her, motherhood is partially responsible for her new, tamer self. "You start thinking of something besides yourself," she says today. "Now my life revolves around my kids . . . It's a gradual process. You don't have a baby and the next day you're different. The more you're with a child, the more you think about things you've never thought about before. It sounds corny, but I worry about the environment, schools, drugs, things every mother worries about."

However, one needn't worry that she is calming

down too far. There still isn't a man alive who can tell her what to do. "I'd've been divorced four times by now if I'd gotten married," she says with regard to her single-parent status. "I just don't think I'm cut out for it. I don't want to have to answer to any guy."

In addition to her life-style changes, she appears to be more focused and in tune with herself than ever before. Whether she's clad in jeans, formal evening gowns, or a Santa Fe chic poncho, the Tanya Tucker of the 1990s is one of country music's most glamorous commodities.

Although she has been a singing star for twenty-two years — she is still younger than half of the other country gals in this book! With her hot nineties hits — including "Soon," "If Your Heart Ain't Busy Tonight," "Down to My Last Teardrop," "It's a Little Too Late," and "Two Sparrows in a Hurricane" — her contemporary career is so solidly based and exciting, it's like she has a new lease on life.

However, Tanya Tucker's life wasn't always so glamorous. Born on October 10, 1958 in Seminole, Texas, the youngest of three children, Tanya always had that something special that separates talented child stars from their siblings. In this world, only dreamers accomplish big things, because they have a goal in mind, and nothing to lose. If that is the case, then her father, Beau Tucker, and her mother, Juanita, must have been as big a pair of dreamers as their daughter Tanya.

The Tucker family drifted from town to town, but the majority of Tanya's early childhood was spent in

Wilcox, Arizona. Beau worked there drilling wells and selling scrap metal. Tanya's older sister, LaCosta, recalls, "We lived in matchboxes, in houses that were literally condemned. We were always trying to work harder." When Tanya was four, and LaCosta was twelve, the two girls began singing around the house, pretending to be The Lennon Sisters. However, it wasn't long before she ditched the Lennons' greatest hits, and found more mature material. By the time she was six, her repertoire was nothing like you'd expect to be coming out of the mouth of a child, as it included Loretta Lynn's "Your Squaw's on the Warpath Tonight" and "Don't Come Home A-Drinkin' With Lovin' on Your Mind." By the time Tanya was nine years old, the family had moved to Phoenix, and she was dead-set on becoming a professional singer. This sounds like a silly children's daydream, however—even at the age of nine—Tanya could sing with power and excitement in her voice.

Tanya's father had the same crazy dreams that his nine-year-old daughter did, and he would drive her all across the countryside to attend concerts by the stars of country music. They would show up at state fairs, and Beau would hoist Tanya up on stage, and there she would be in the spotlight with the likes of Mel Tillis, or whoever else was headlining that particular day.

The family was living in a trailer in Utah the day Beau headed to Las Vegas to see if his luck at the casinos could raise enough money to make a demo tape of little thirteen-year-old Tanya. When he arrived home he displayed his winnings of $1,100. He loaded Tanya into the car, and they drove back to Vegas that very night. After three hours in a recording studio he had rented, Beau and Tanya left the studio with six songs on tape. Recalls Tanya, "We had about forty bucks to get home on."

Now, at long last, Beau had something on tape to send to record companies. After sending out dozens of tapes, Beau finally struck a deal with Nashville producer Billy Sherill. It was through a successful Las Vegas songwriter, Dolores Fuller, that the introduction to Sherill came from. In 1972 Columbia Records released Tanya Tucker's first single, "Delta Dawn," and she immediately hit the jackpot when the song sailed up the country music charts. In 1973 and 1974, Tanya racked up a surprising number of hits, including "What's Your Mother's Name," "Blood Red and Goin' Down," "Would You Lay Me Down (In a Field of Stone)," and "The Man That Turned My Mother On."

At the age of fifteen she was on the cover of *Rolling Stone* magazine, with the headline "Hi, I'm Tanya Tucker, I'm 15, You're Gonna Hear from Me" spattered on the page next to her photo. In 1975 she shifted to MCA Records, where she would stay until the end of the decade. She scored with country albums like the "Gold" certified *Tanya Tucker* (1975), *Lovin' and Learnin'* (1976) and *Here's Some Love* (1976).

One of Tanya's flings during this era was with the yet-to-be-famous Don Johnson. According to her,

"Me and Donny hung out for about a year and a half when I lived in L.A. I'd have to pay for gas for his little beat-up VW. We had a lot of fun times and fought a lot because we were both very, very young and living on the edge."

In 1978 Tanya made a huge switch in her career, by shifting from country music to straightforward rock & roll. She parted company with long-time producer Jerry Crutchfield, and hired Jerry Goldstein of Far Out Productions. Goldstein and Tucker worked together to try and transform her into a female Elvis Presley. The results can be heard on the exciting album *T-N-T*, which was certified "Gold" and became a huge cross-over smash. The single version of Buddy Holly's "Not Fade Away" even proved to be a pop hit for Tanya. Another cut on the album, "Save Me," she wrote with Goldstein, and it was released to raise money and awareness about the annual slaughter of over 200,000 baby seals in Canada's Magdale Islands. Just to play it safe, the album also included a country song called "Texas (When I Die)." Other than that, *T-N-T* was a rock explosion. Presley had just died that August, so Tucker included her own version of "Heartbreak Hotel" on the album as a tribute to him.

Since the beginning of her career, Tanya had been fascinated with Presley. According to her, "I wanted to be just like him, I grew up with him in my heart." She also became close friends with Mae Axton, who wrote the song "Heartbreak Hotel" for Elvis in 1956. (Mae's also songwriter/actor Hoyt Axton's mother.) According to Mae, "Tanya adored Elvis. I slipped him in one time to see her [perform], and didn't let her know, because I thought it would make her go to pieces. And he made the remark, he says, 'Well, you know Mae, she's kind of a female Elvis Presley.' "

The album's cover photo of twenty-year-old Tanya was almost as hotly received as was her new rock sound. On *T-N-T* she is shown standing in front of several cases of explosives, in black leather pants and spike heels, pulling the microphone cord between her legs like she was doing a bump-and-grind routine with a feather boa. On the album's centerfold, she was shown clad in backless red spandex, with six sticks of dynamite in her hand. When *The New York Times* reviewed the album they pointed out that on it Tanya's singing blended "the emotional urgency of Tammy Wynette with the grit and power of blues-rocker Bonnie Raitt."

On December 13, 1978, MCA Records threw a cocktail party for Tanya in New York City at the restaurant One Fifth Avenue, which included among its guests, members of The Village People, and the who's who of the Manhattan press (including this author!). That night at The Bottom Line in Greenwich Village, dressed in a skintight black body suit, Tanya showed the Big Apple what her new rock image was all about.

According to her at the time, "I feel there's a basic country music just as there is a basic rock & roll. I want to sing my own music which is somewhere in the middle. This album is really not a big change, though people come up to me and tell me it is. They also say it's something I should have done a long time ago, but it wasn't meant to happen then. But it is something that has been happening."

Encouraged by the reception with which *T-N-T* was met, the following year Tanya recorded her follow-up rock album, *Tear Me Apart*. This time around she went with producer Mike Chapman who was fresh from producing "Heart of Glass" and "Rapture" for Debbie Harry and Blondie, and Pat Benatar's "If You Think You Know How to Love Me." The album was much more successful at dragging Tanya into the wailing guitars of rock & roll, and didn't include a single country cut.

By 1981 Tanya was back in the country realm, largely due to her widely publicized affair with Glen Campbell, who at the time was approximately twice her age. Their rowdy partying and public fights were legendary. As recently as 1991 Tucker was still bitter. According to her, it was a "matter of me being too young and him being a little too messed up. He doesn't talk to me, but I'd talk to him." She further stated, "And I'm tired of him blaming all that shit on me. He's come on TV and blamed me and I don't want to hear no more of that. When he talks about me, he'd better have a smile on his face because I don't go around persecuting him, which I very well could. It was a phase of my life and I'm through it and I don't want to hear him blaming me for anything because he *was* twice my age. By God, he should know the difference."

However, while they were still an item, Tanya released her *Should I Do It* album, with the Tucker/ Campbell duet cut "Shoulder By Shoulder" on it. The title song from that album became a huge hit for Tanya, and the publicity from that affair didn't hurt. The hysterical thing about the song is the fact that on the song "Shoulder To Shoulder" Tanya and Glen are lyrically singing about fondly looking back on their long and happy life together, twenty years in the future. Ironically, their affair didn't last twenty months—let alone twenty years!

In 1982 Tanya dumped Glen, and left MCA Records. That year she released her aptly titled Arista debut album *Changes*. The pleasant album was a blend of light country, pop, with a touch of rock. Tanya tackled the Barbara Lewis 1960s pop hit "Baby I'm Yours," and got decidedly autobiographical on the ballad of lost love, "Changes" which she co-wrote. She also scored a hit with the song "Feel Right."

There was a three-year gap in Tanya's recording career after her Arista album. For a while her personal life kept her in the press more than her recordings. Just as she always had, Tanya continued to tour around the country, averaging over 200 concert dates a year. Life on the road, she claims, became her physical downfall. She seemed to be drinking and partying a bit excessively when she was off stage. According to her, "You leave your place where you're performing, leave the adoration and go to your hotel room and you sit there. And pretty soon you're goin' downstairs callin' the guys in the band—'Let's party!'

To curb the loneliness was the biggest reason I did it."

Tanya ended her absence from the recording studios by signing with Capitol Records and their Liberty label in 1986. She re-connected with producer Jerry Crutchfield, and they began producing a successive string of hits, one after another. Their eighties collaborations included "One Love at a Time," "Just Another Love," "I Won't Take Less Than Your Love" (with Paul Overstreet and Paul Davis), "Strong Enough to Bend," and "Highway Robbery."

Meanwhile, Tanya's parents and friends were becoming concerned with her drinking and partying habits. Using "tough love" tactics, they forcibly checked her into the Betty Ford Center in early 1988. "I'm not saying I had a problem," she explains, "but I'm glad I went. It was a trying experience. I just loved to have fun, and at the time, that was what you had fun with [cocaine]. Now it's not in vogue."

After her stay at the Betty Ford Center, Tanya returned her concentration to her career. After a concert in Tulsa, Oklahoma, she met a twenty-three-year-old actor named Ben Reed. They hit it off, and she invited him to appear in one of her upcoming videos. It wasn't long before the sparks of love flew. On October 10, 1988 — Tanya's thirtieth birthday — she was in Nashville to appear on the Country Music Awards. That was the night Tanya claims that her daughter, Presley, was conceived. However, she and Ben had a huge fight that night, and he left town in the morning. Since that time, her relationship has been "off" and "on."

When she found out that she was pregnant, Tanya decided that she was going to keep her baby. Needless to say, her parents, and all of her business advisers were all up in arms about this latest bombshell, and the effects that it could have on her career. Recalls Tanya, "I had to go into this meeting. The president of my record label was there, my publicist, my agent, my dad, my producer, all these men sitting around saying, 'Okay, how are *we* gonna handle this?' It was awful."

How she decided to handle it was to just have her baby, and let the chips fall where they may. According to her, she had nothing to hide: "This was the guy I was gonna marry and be with forever. Things didn't happen that way. It's not a perfect world."

Tanya gave birth to her daughter, Presley, on July 5, 1989, but she did not marry Ben Reed. Said Tanya at the time, "My deal is I don't want it to be like we're back together because of Presley. I want us to be together because we want to be together."

Tucker continued with her usual touring schedule after Presley was born, simply taking the baby on the road with her. Reed would occasionally visit Tanya and Presley. During one of the visits in 1991, Tanya became pregnant again, and in October of that year she gave birth to a son, Beau Grayson. She simply said, "I wanted my little girl to have a full-blooded brother."

Although Tanya and Ben remain close friends—who have two children together—she still plays the field. In 1993 she proclaimed, "I can't find anything wrong with Ben—there are many women who would die for him." However, she says, "Something's missing. I'm not saying it has to be missing forever. I used to think that if you weren't in love now, forget it. But now I know love can grow." Simultaneously, she has been dating twenty-four-year-old Matt Thurson, heir to a fried-chicken fortune. According to her, neither man is "Mr. Right" in her book: "What I'm looking for is a John Wayne kind of guy."

While the soap opera that is Tanya's personal life continued to turn, her career suddenly turned hot in 1990. She had been producing sporadic hit singles in the late eighties, but suddenly country music was "in," and she found herself right in the middle of it all. When she released her *Tennessee Woman* album in 1990, she hit number one with the single "Walkin' Shoes," and also scored big with "Don't Go Out" (duet with T. Graham Brown) and "It Won't Be Me." Based on the success of that album, Tanya was named the Country Music Association's Female Vocalist of the Year in 1991. When her name was called that night at the awards show at the Grand Ole Opry, she received a huge standing ovation. Suddenly, after all of those years of career twists and turns, Tanya Tucker was Nashville's comeback queen.

According to her, "Everybody kept comin' up to me and sayin', 'I was the first one standing!' People that don't even know me tell me their whole family was screaming, running around the house, acting like crazy people when they announced my name. They said everybody in the press room just stood up and went nuts. They said no other award got that kind of reaction. And then the standing ovation was just the topper. To me that was, I hate to say, better than the award."

Also in 1991, Tanya released her certified "Gold" *What Do I Do with Me* album. It contained the number-one hit "Down to My Last Teardrop," and the smashes "If Your Heart Ain't Busy Tonight," "Some Kind of Trouble," and "(Without You) What Do I Do about Me." Suddenly she was on a roll.

In 1992 came her album *Can't Run from Yourself,* which was almost instantly certified "Gold." The song "Two Sparrows in a Hurricane" sailed up to number one, and she also had huge hits with "It's a Little Too Late" and "Tell Me about It" (duet with Delbert McClinton). She was on such a hot streak, that her record company felt compelled to release her twenty-sixth album *Tanya Tucker's Greatest Hits 1990-1992* to capitalize on the sudden resurgence of her popularity.

Her latest album, *Soon* (1993), perpetuated her "Gold" streak. The smash title cut, about professing love via a telephone answering machine—in the Top Ten at year's end—was the perfect way to start off 1994. She also released the video cassette, *Tanya Tucker's Country Workout* (1993), an exercise tape set to her music. In October 1993, when the "Double Platinum" number one album *Common Thread: Songs of The Eagles* was released, with country stars singing classic Eagles songs, Tanya Tucker was right there with her version of "Already Gone." The funny thing is the fact that Tanya was covering songs by The Eagles two decades ago, when she recorded "After the Thrill Is Gone" on her 1976 *Lovin' and Learnin'* album. Clearly, she was several years ahead of her time when it came to picking hits!

Although she now has her two children in tow wherever she goes, Tanya still wows audiences on stage from coast to coast. Describing her legendary on-stage excitement, Tanya says, "The best word these days is 'energy.' I like to move around on stage — I always have. I always felt very motivated to move. And when my music moves me, I feel like movin' and I really can't stand still."

Tanya Tucker in the 1990s is on the most thrilling and successful winning streak of her career, and she isn't about to let up one little bit. Even during the periods when her record chart activity was slow, her personal life kept her name out there. According to her, "At times when I didn't have records out, the press has really kept me out there. My bad reputation has done wonderful things for me!" Twenty-two years since she burst onto the country music scene, Tanya Tucker is better, hotter, and sexier than ever before. And, this is clearly just the beginning of big things for this gorgeous bundle of country dynamite!

Chapter Fifteen
Dolly Parton

Dolly Parton's career has had more ups and down than the roller coaster at Dollywood. She stands only five feet tall without her usual five-inch high-heel shoes on. Her own hair is always buried underneath one of her hundreds of mountainous blond wigs. Her fingernails are sculptured talons of candy-apple red, and her laughter is a heartfelt fun-loving cackle.

Of all the women who are hot on the country charts in the 1990s, Parton is the one with the longest-lasting career. Although her career originally started with her as a country singer and songwriter, over the years she has grown and expanded to also become a TV star, a movie star, and a pop singer as well. By 1989, Dolly had gotten so far off the tracks from her country-singing career, that she has had to make a concentrated effort to get back into the country scene, and to capture some of the growing audience that nineties country music now reaches.

With her three certified "Gold" Columbia country albums, *White Limozeen* (1989), *Eagle When She Flies* (1991), and *Slow Dancing with the Moon* (1993), she has reestablished herself as a force in today's country music. Her recent hits "Romeo," and the number-ones "Yellow Roses," "Why'd You Come in Here Lookin' Like That" and "Rockin' Years" (with Ricky Van Shelton) have put the country music spotlight back on her. When her *Eagle When She Flies* album was also certified "Platinum," it marked the fourth time she had a million-selling LP in her long career. She was already on a winning streak when Whitney Houston took Dolly's song "I'll Always Love You," and turned it into a number-one hit in 1993. Suddenly Dolly's songwriting talents were exposed to an even wider audience.

As 1994 got underway, Dolly Parton was as busy as a bumblebee in a spring garden. On September 1993's *Country Music Association Awards* presentation, she and country legends Loretta Lynn and Tammy Wynette debuted "Silver Threads And Golden Needles," a cut from their long-awaited triumvirate album, *Honky Tonk Angels*. Not long afterward, it was announced that her next album project was to be *Trio II*—a musical reunion with Linda Ronstadt and Emmylou Harris. Dolly was also heard on four additional 1993 albums: she sang the song "Billy

Dale" on Asleep At The Wheel's *Tribute To Bob Wills & The Texas Playboys* disc, "If You Ain't Got Love" from the soundtrack to the movie *The Beverly Hillbillies,* she and Neil Diamond performed "You've Lost That Lovin' Feelin' " on his *Up On The Roof* album, and she and James Ingram dueted on the song "The Day I Fall In Love" from the *Beethoven's 2nd* soundtrack album.

In December of 1993 it was announced that Dolly would again take on network television, with the sitcom *Dixie Fixin's.* With writers from *Married With Children* involved, and as a joint venture between CBS-TV and Disney TV, it stars Parton as the host of a Chicago cable TV cooking show, with a fall 1994 premiere date.

In the past twenty years, Dolly Parton has turned herself from a country singer with a cult following, into a multi-media industry. In addition to being a singing star, she also runs her own production company, owns an amusement park, a Hollywood mansion, macadamia-nut groves in Hawaii, and a Tennessee mountain home.

As glorious as her present life is, equally unexotic was her upbringing in the Smoky Mountains of Tennessee in the 1940s. Born the fourth of twelve children to a mountain man and his young wife, Dolly Rebecca Dennison's only hint that she might one day become a world-famous singing star came in her elaborate daydreams.

The tiny cabin that Dolly grew up in had no running water, nor electricity.

According to her, "I lived in fairy tales and storybooks, and I knew that we were missing a lot that I saw in books, but we were real happy. You see, Mom and Dad stayed together. We had our problems. Daddy, he often ran around and he had some children outside of us, but he was a good father and a good husband. He always came home. He was just a little wild, and I can certainly understand that, because I'm a combination of both of them. But he always loved Mama and always treated us good. It was hard times. Mama was sick a lot and there were a lot of depressing times. What was good about it was we lived out in the country. We were very close to nature and free to grow up the way we did. We didn't have cars to get hit by, we didn't have neighbors to get raped by, we just lived way out in the woods. We lived close to God and close to nature. I think coming out of that gave us a real good solid foundation, a good wholesome attitude."

She also knew that she was never going to grow up to have the kind of life that she saw in the back woods. "I certainly loved my mother and my aunts and sisters and all those people up there," she recalls. "But I never had any intention of being like them when I grew up, living by those kind of rules. I never planned on staying home with kids, devoted to one man. And when I first started getting attention by being able to sing and play the guitar and people started responding—well, it was like I fell in love."

Dolly began writing her own poems and songs at the age of seven. Thanks to her Uncle Bill, she traveled to Nashville, and at the age of ten she recorded and released her first record—the single "Puppy Love" on Gold Band Records (1956). At fifteen she made her second recording, for Mercury Records—a lamenting country ditty called "It May Not Kill Me, But It's Sure Gonna Hurt." After that, she was hooked on the idea of a recording career. In 1964 she became the first member of her family ever to graduate from high school. Her commencement exercises were held on a Friday, and by Saturday evening she had moved to Nashville to seek her fortune in the music business.

According to Dolly, she knew that she had to go after her dreams. "I had such faith," she says, "I believed so strongly that it could not *not* happen. You can think yourself sick or well, you can also think yourself successful. It all started with a good attitude. A feeling of, 'I don't know why I can't do it. This is America. They can't put me in jail for trying.' I figured, 'I can't be any poorer than I've been at home. So to be poor in the city, what's the difference?' "

She had arrived in Nashville in a dirty outfit, so she went into the Why Washy laundromat. It was right there that she met the man she was going to marry—Carl Dean.

Thanks to the encouragement and guidance of her uncle Bill Owens, Dolly soon found fame as a country music songwriter. In 1966 Bill Phillips had a hit with her song "Put It Off Until Tomorrow." She signed her own recording contract with Monument Records in the mid-sixties and produced her own Top Ten hit, "Dumb Blonde."

In 1968 Dolly signed up with Porter Wagoner as her manager and her singing partner. As a duet, Porter and Dolly recorded several hit albums in the late 1960s and the early 1970s. Simultaneously, Dolly began her own solo recording career with RCA Records in Nashville. In 1970 Dolly received her first TV exposure as a regular on Porter Wagoner's syndicated television show bearing his name.

In the early 1970s Dolly's compositions and her recordings began to reach a broader audience than most country singers had ever received. When the folk/rock sounds of Melanie, Linda Ronstadt, Maria Muldaur, and Joni Mitchell became popular during this era, the country purity of Dolly's music was perfect to break out of the "hillbilly music" stamp with which country songs were previously labeled. In 1974 Maria Muldaur recorded Dolly's song "My Tennessee Mountain

Home," and that same year Parton's own hit "Jolene" crossed over to the pop charts. With this huge taste of success, Dolly realized she wanted to break through to a broader market, and she left Porter Wagoner as her singing partner, and she fired him as her manager. It was also that year that she first released the song "I Will Always Love You," which went to number one on the country music charts.

According to Dolly, it was Wagoner who inspired the song "I Will Always Love You." Says she, "I wrote the song about my relationship and my leaving Porter Wagoner. That was in the very early seventies, and I was trying to leave his show, and he was suing me and we were having lots of trouble. I was heartbroken, and so was he. And I was trying to say, 'Hey, look — if I was to stay, I'd just be in the way. I've got dreams. I want to go to other things. But I'll always love you, and I'll always appreciate you.' So I thought, well, this was my way of saying this, in a song."

It was in 1975 that a magical triumvirate was born. When Linda Ronstadt recorded her hit album *Prisoner in Disguise,* on it she included Dolly's "I Will Always Love You." One of Linda's recording-star friends, Emmylou Harris, appeared on the same Ronstadt album, singing harmony vocals on the song "The Sweetest Gift." When Linda and Emmylou started talking, they both agreed that Dolly Parton was their favorite singer. When the three ladies finally got together, they decided they would make a dynamite singing trio. To test their musical harmony, in 1977 they recorded several songs for a proposed trio album. Unfortunately, record company conflicts and opposing career obligations prevented the album's completion for ten years. A couple of the cuts did however surface on Emmylou and Linda's albums. Says Harris, "In those first sessions we did 'Mister Sandman,' 'When Cowgirls Get Blue,' 'Evangeline,' 'My Blue Tears,' and a few other things. We tried to do it in ten days. It was difficult, but I'm amazed at how much we did get done."

According to Dolly, "We had problems, because we were all three on different labels. Everybody thought it was such a spectacular idea. Everybody was pushing and shoving us, trying to get it done for business reasons. And we thought, 'Well, we want to do it and do something great, and if it sells, wonderful, and if it don't . . .' They were really thinking only money, and we were thinking 'creativity.' "

In the meantime, Dolly starred in her own half-hour syndicated TV series called "Dolly," and she formed and later disbanded her own concert troupe called the Travelin' Family Band. In 1978 something explosive happened when Dolly released a song called "Here You Come

Again," and it became her first Top Ten pop million-seller. From that point on, Dolly Parton's career has been a mixture of country stylings teamed with crossover pop/rock tunes.

Hit singles including "Two Doors Down," "Heartbreaker," and "Baby I'm Burning" catapulted Parton's *Heartbreaker* album to million-selling "Platinum" status, and a Grammy Award for "Here You Come Again" followed. In 1979 Dolly signed a contract for her movie debut opposite Jane Fonda and Lily Tomlin in *9 to 5*. When the film was released at the end of 1980, word was suddenly out: Dolly Parton had instantly become a movie star!

While *9 to 5* was selling tickets like hotcakes at the box-office, Dolly and Burt Reynolds were signed to star in the screen adaptation of the Broadway hit musical *The Best Little Whorehouse in Texas*. In February 1981 Dolly won two more Grammy Awards — for her number-one hit song *9 to 5*. She also won an Academy Award nomination for the same composition.

The filming of *The Best Little Whorehouse in Texas* became a behind-the-scenes fiasco. Battles over the script broke out — with the stars: Parton and Reynolds on one side; and Larry L. King, the author of the book of the Broadway show, on the other side. King claimed that Dolly and Burt were changing the core story for their own vanity, and the disgruntled writer even published his own condemning book, entitled "The Whorehouse Papers" (Viking Press). When *The Best Little Whorehouse in Texas* was released in 1982, the critics ripped into it with a vengeance. However, the names of Dolly Parton and Burt Reynolds on the marquees guaranteed ticket sales throughout middle America. Cleverly, Parton insisted on including her song "I Will Always Love You" in the film, and she again released it as a single, and turned it into a hit for herself a second time. Dolly, who was paid $1,500,000 plus a percentage for playing the part of whorehouse owner Miss Mona, was in the position to call her own career shots. Her next film choice however, proved faulty.

Dolly's subsequent movie performance was in the ill-chosen *Rhinestone* with Sylvester Stallone. When it was released in 1984, it was a bona fide bomb, both critically and financially.

Fortunately, Dolly's next partnership venture proved golden. Teaming up with Kenny Rogers in 1983 for a duet song called "Islands in the Stream" launched them to the top of the record charts. They made such a successful team that in 1984 they hit the concert circuit and headlined America's biggest stadiums and concert halls. While their second smash duet, "Real Love," was hitting the Top Ten, Dolly's health began to fail. When she bowed out of the concert tour in the middle of it, the press began to question whether

her recurring throat problems signaled the end of her singing career. These throat problems came on the heels of a gynecological and intestinal illness that had left her unable to bear children. With such serious illnesses befalling her in rapid succession, Dolly's fans began to worry that she was caught up in a spiraling physical decline.

While she recuperated from surgery for her "female problems," she remained active on the record charts, releasing the albums *Burlap & Satin,* her fifties/sixties rock-tribute LP *The Great Pretender,* the *Rhinestone* soundtrack, and the "Platinum" holiday album *Once Upon A Christmas* with Kenny Rogers.

After *9 to 5* had become a huge number-one pop hit for Dolly, she began to de-countryize her musical image. In 1981 she had even turned the rock classic "House of the Rising Sun" into a hit for herself. Her album "The Great Pretender" was 100 percent rock & roll. Some of her country fans were miffed by this move, but Dolly maintains that she wasn't about to stand still when it comes to her own creative development. "Music was my world and my job, but it was the music *business,"* she stresses. "I pissed a lot of people off when I decided to make a change, but I knew I had gone as far as I could in the country music field . . . I wanted to go out into the world. I wanted to do movies. I wanted to cross over. I was a personality. I had the freedom, and

I saw no reason not to do it."

In 1986 the world saw the emergence of a sleeker new Dolly Parton—forty pounds lighter than her former self. In January of that year she turned forty, and she feted herself by buying a plush Hollywood mansion. In May 1986, Dolly's $20,000,000 dream amusement park, Dollywood, opened to the public. Located near her birthplace in rural Pigeon Forge, Tennessee, Parton's Dollywood witnessed a booming percentage of profits in its first season of operation.

In December 1986, Dolly starred in her first made-for-TV movie, "A Down-Home Christmas." A charming Christmas fable, the movie did well in the ratings, and it proved to television networks that Parton was a genuine TV draw. Soon afterward, plans began to be drawn up for her to headline her own TV series.

In 1987, Dolly found herself at the high point of her international popularity. She began the year with the release of her long-awaited million-selling *Trio* album with Linda Ronstadt and Emmylou Harris. The trio appeared in two videos that were filmed by George Lucas, and the LP won them a Grammy Award.

With regard to the evolution of the *Trio* album, Emmylou Harris recalls, "Linda called in November of '85 and asked if I had thought about doing the project. I had a lot of time available in '86 because I wasn't going on the road much. So, I called Dolly. We met in Nashville to pick a producer and the time when we would record. We picked some of the songs. Linda thought it should be done acoustically. Dolly and I agreed. The other album we wanted to do [in 1978] was sort of rock & roll. But we decided to do an acoustic album of really sweet stuff that really shows off the fact that we love to sing together—not to put a lot of production on it. We started on Dolly's birthday, the 19th of January [1986]."

Says Ronstadt, "We planned and rehearsed it in Nashville and ended up recording it in Los Angeles. Emmylou dug up a lot of the material, and there are some Dolly Parton originals, as well as songs Dolly learned from her mother. Most of the songs predate bluegrass. Unlike bluegrass, the music is quiet, intimate parlor music intended to be appreciated by the people playing it."

"Through the years," said Dolly, "we noticed that every time we got together, we'd always tend to sing real country songs. Linda and Emmy'd say, 'Oh, sing us that ol' song "Your Mama Said," or one of those old country songs.' It always seemed that the simpler the song was, the better we'd sound. So, that just seemed to dictate what we should do: a simpler, traditional album." When *Trio* was released, it became a high point in each of the three women's musical careers.

Meanwhile, as a solo artist, Dolly moved to Columbia Records. According to her contract, she planned on recording one country album a year, and one pop/rock album a year. That fall she released her first album for Columbia, entitled *Rainbow*. It contained the hit single "The River Unbroken," and a duet with Smokey Robinson called "I Know You by Heart."

When ABC-TV announced in early 1987 that Dolly would be starring in her own weekly variety television show, there were more than a few skeptics who felt that she wouldn't be able to pull it off successfully. First of all, there hadn't been a "variety" show on network television since "Barbara Mandrell & The Mandrell Sisters" left the air in June of 1982. Network executives said that variety songs were "dead." There were others who just didn't think that Dolly could pull it off. She set out to prove them wrong.

To start with, Dolly began the project with the iron-clad contract to end them all. In it, ABC-TV agreed to pay her $44,000,000, with a two-season, forty-four show commitment. In other words, "Dolly" was the million-dollar series that theoretically could not be canceled without the mutual consent of Parton and ABC-TV. The show debuted on September 27, 1987.

For the first episode of "Dolly," Parton welcomed guest stars Pee Wee Herman, Oprah Winfrey, and Dudley Moore. Predictably, the musical segments were the strongest parts of the show, and the comedy sketches were the lightest. There were also several spots on the show in which Dolly's fans were seen on videotape, making comments, and lavishing praise on the show's star. The debut program astonished everyone when it was rated by Nielsen as the number-five show in that week's line-up.

There was a segment on the show called "Dolly's Date," in which a different unannounced mystery man would show up at Dolly's stage set living room door. Until she opened the door, the audience had no idea who Dolly's date would be. Among her mystery dates during the series were Burt Reynolds, Patrick Duffy, and Dudley Moore. It was a cute idea, but about two minutes into the skit, it usually died.

"Dixie's Diner" was one of the most winning recurring skits in those first episodes. In that series, Dolly played the part of Dixie, the proprietress of a roadside diner. The character was one she could comfortably become: a combination waitress and confidante who could serve up pie and advice at the same time.

Since she had lost so much weight before the show went on the air, trimming herself down to a slim 100 pounds, there was an instant attempt to do the whole Cher-like high-fashion trip with her. While Bob Mackie made Cher a visual TV star in the 1970s; Tony Chase was brought in to work his bugle-beaded magic with Dolly. She wore the outrageous fashions well, but wasn't always at ease with what her producers were having her do when she was all decked out in gowns and wigs.

The first show got off to a huge start. Beginning with its initial episode in the Top 10 of the Nielsen ratings, it was only a matter of weeks before it was lingering in the bottom third of the prime-time network ratings. The program suddenly became a very expensive "dress rehearsal." Each week the producers would be trying to change and alter the concept of the show, and it wasn't long before the entire program became a disastrous muddle of contradicting elements. Was the show country? Pop/rock? Comedy? Variety? It soon became a nightmare which never remained the same format of a show from week to a week, and instead of appealing to a widely diverse number of audiences, it eluded everyone.

According to Dolly, "They [the producers] had me doing songs like 'Someone to Watch over Me.' That's like Barbra Streisand singing 'Don't Come Home A-Drinkin'.'" Indeed, it wasn't working, and after everyone tuned in to the premiere episode, the show took a ratings dive. By November, the show was in serious trouble, and weekly changes began to take place. For the Thanksgiving week episode, the cast and crew of the show flew to Tennessee for a "home for the holidays" show. It made a temporary upswing, ranking twenty-sixth in the Nielsens, however, by January, it had fallen to number 51, and the network moved the show from Sunday nights to Saturdays. On her Saturday debut, January 16, 1988, Dolly pulled out the big guns and had Kenny Rogers on the show to give the episode some added excitement. To pull the show farther away from the Hollywood slick look of the initial episodes, Dolly then hired a team of Southern writers who were more in tune with her roots as a country performer. Actor Charles Durning joined the series as a regular character when the show moved to Saturday nights. Finally, by the end of the season, both Dolly and ABC-TV agreed to cancel the show.

Dolly turned her focus to other aspects of her career—namely her country-music career, and her stalled movie career. She ended up with hot new hits in both categories.

In 1989 she released the album *White Limozeen,* which was produced by Ricky Skaggs. It was her first totally country album in years that didn't try and ride the fence between country and pop. She certainly had proven that she is capable of being successful at singing to both audiences, but when she began releasing albums that contained country, pop, *and* rock songs, she seemed to lose her focus.

Her role in the 1989 movie *Steel Magnolias*

marked one of her most successful screen performances. Playing a gossipy Southern hairdresser,
Parton shared the screen with Julia Roberts,
Olympia Dukakis, Shirley McLaine, Daryl Han-
nah, and Sally Field. The prestigious production
helped to fulfill the promise of a successful acting career that *9 to 5* had predicted. Since that
time she has starred in the made-for-TV movie
"Wild Texas Wind" (1991) about a country singer
in an abusive relationship, and the film *Straight
Talk* (1992). In the latter film, Parton plays a
woman who is mistaken for a radio station callin psychologist, and finds herself behind the microphone, dishing out more country common
sense than Freudian learning. Co-starring James
Woods, the film was a fun confection, which allowed Dolly to play her own charming self to a
tee.

Viewing her own film career, Parton ponders,
"Well, I think *9 to 5* was special, because it was
the first one and it was a big success. I thought
that all the movies would be that easy. But they
are not. I think my very personal favorite right
now is *Straight Talk,* which kind of summed up
my personal thinking. I think if anybody didn't
know me in my lifetime — nieces and nephews
and younger ones — if I should die or something,
they could see that movie and see more about
who I really am than in anything else I've done."

When the 1989 album *White Limozeen* successfully returned Dolly to the country-music charts, she decided to concentrate on that particular side of her career. On 1991's *Eagle When She Flies* album she teamed up with Ricky Van Shelton on "Rocking Years," and with Lorrie Morgan on the song "Best Woman Wins."

Since that album was such a smash, Dolly took the formula of having hot new country guest stars to a further degree on her 1993 *Slow Dancing With the Moon* album. Billy Dean sings with Dolly on the duet "(You Got Me Over) A Heartache Tonight," and Collin Raye shared the microphone with her on "Whenever Forever Comes." Other guest stars included Vince Gill, Rodney Crowell, Lari White, Ricky Skaggs, Alison Krauss, Marty Stuart, Emmylou Harris, Chet Atkins, and Jo-El Sonnier.

However, the all-star event to end them all came on the song "Romeo." The song is a virtual "girls' night out" featuring Dolly singing with Tanya Tucker, Mary-Chapin Carpenter, Kathy Mattea, Pam Tillis — and Billy Ray Cyrus as *the* Romeo himself. Explains Parton, "I wrote the song originally about my little nephew, Brian, and he's kind of a little Romeo. So I've been calling him Romeo for several months; he don't keep up with his schoolwork, and he's in love with all the girls, and all the girls are in love with him. So one morning I started writing this song, and since I knew my nephew didn't sing, I thought of Billy Ray singing the part on the album. So I called him up, and I said, 'Lord, you're the best Romeo I know in this business, so would you like to play the part of Romeo in my video?' So then I gathered up Kathy Mattea and Mary-Chapin Carpenter and Tanya Tucker and Pam Tillis, and we donated the money from the single to the Red Cross. We just wanted to do something that was tongue-in-cheek and fun."

When the album was released, Dolly made no bones about her motives for having all of the hot new country guest stars on her album. "I did this album with younger artists, so it wouldn't be overlooked," she admitted. "I thought, 'I'm going to do everything I can to make this as mainstream as I can and as up-to-date as I can'—and, because most of these young people idolize the older people in the business, every single person I asked was thrilled to be on the record. I thought, 'If that's the only way I can get a record played, I'll just hang on to their coattails!' "

One of the songs on the album, Dolly's composition "High and Mighty," is a knock-out gospel number. She has visions of expanding it into a film. "People are scared, they're frightened with all the stuff that's going on, and they're looking for hope," she says. "That's one of the reasons I'm trying to pull together a show right now called 'The High And Mighty,' a movie-of-the-week where a famous star goes into the ministry. It's sort of an uplifting, gospel kind of show that I'm hoping to run off into a series as well."

According to her, several of the songs on this new album are of personal significance. One of them even speaks of her return to the country-music arena. "There's a song on my new album called 'Full Circle,' " she says. "I feel like I have come full circle. There was a period of time when I did records that meant nothing to me nor to anyone else. But I was trying things I had the opportunity to try."

When the album was released, Dolly drew rave reviews. *Time* magazine proclaimed, "*Slow Dancing with the Moon* is an ideal reminder of Parton's status as a premier singer/songwriter." *Country America* announced, "This is Dolly's rig all the way. She's the queen bee of this hive of Nashville honey; she's glad to be home, and it shows." *USA Today* glowed, "Sheer pleasure . . . who else can sing so sweetly and simply and strongly as Dolly Parton? Nobody." And, *People* magazine applauded, "It's great to hear her singing as joyfully as she does . . . she's come full circle indeed."

In 1993, when Whitney Houston turned Dolly's song "I Will Always Love You" into the longest running number-one hit in the history of the pop charts, Parton was pleased as punch.

"My God, she's set me up for life," Dolly exclaims—tallying up all of her songwriter's royalties. "If you're lucky enough in your life to get two or three songs like that, you literally can retire."

Referring to the message in the song, Dolly feels that it's the songwriter's task to express emotions that others cannot verbalize. "It's my responsibility," she claims. "Because not everybody has the gift of writing, but they all do have the gift of feeling. And I think that's what's so wonderful about music—music speaks with the voice of the soul. And if you are able to write . . . like 'I Will Always Love You,' the song Whitney Houston has out, that I wrote twenty years ago, the way that song has touched people—[more than] six million copies—because it's something simply said. Everybody wants to say that to somebody, whether it's your children going away to college or you've broken up with a partner or you're breaking up with a lover or a husband or a wife. You want that person to say that they hope you have a good life and you get everything you want and, 'I will always love you.' Simple words, but people don't know how to say those things."

Not only does Dolly Parton know how to express emotions in a song, she also knows how to make savvy business decisions as well. In 1993 *People* magazine ranked her the fifth richest female entertainer in show business today. (The list is of "estimated worth," and ran as follows: Oprah Winfrey—$200 million, Mary Tyler Moore—$125 million, Madonna—$100 million, Barbra Streisand—$100 million, Dolly—$7O million.) According to her, "I'm not out to pretend I'm not out to make as good a living as I can. I'm a business-minded woman. I always tell my accountants, my managers, my bankers or agents: 'I don't need advice, I need information. *I* will make my own decisions.' "

Probably one of the most outrageous trademarks of Dolly Parton's is her look, and her image itself. In the song "White Limozeen" she laughingly refers to herself as looking like the cartoon character Daisy Mae in Hollywood. That is probably the most apt description around. "Sure, I look like a cartoon," she admits. "But you know, it started out very honest and sincere, and it still is, basically. I don't mean to look trashy and whore-y, it's just that I don't think I do. And even if I do look like a whore, I sure don't feel like one. I just can't stand to look plain, 'cause that don't fit my personality. I may be a very artificial-looking person, but the good news is, I'm very real on the inside. All the rest is just like dressing up in your mama's clothes and playing with paints. It makes me feel shiny and sparkly and new. It just makes me want to get out and do things."

One of the most interesting aspects of Dolly's

personal life is the fact that she is still married
to Carl Dean. The odd part of the union is the
fact that Dolly spends the majority of her time
in Hollywood, and Dean stays in Tennessee. De-
fensively she states, "Listen, my husband is not
the type to hang onto my skirttail, trying to pull
me back. He doesn't want me in his face all the
time, nor do I want to be in his. We're both free
to work and free to live. If he hadn't married
me, I think he would have been some old hermit
somewhere, living up in the woods in a cabin,
'cause he don't care about seeing people. He
likes his privacy. So I just do my socializing
other places."

With all of this talk about Dolly returning to
country music, and focusing on that, don't think
that she doesn't still have her fingers in dozens
of pies. "I wake with new dreams every day," she
claims, "so it's really hard for me to say exactly
what's left. I know one thing I've wanted to do
for a long time that I'm finally doing — I'm starting my own cosmetic line. I've always wanted to
do that, and I've always wanted to finish my
Broadway Southern musical."

Dolly Parton is a dreamer. A flamboyant, outrageous, warm, sincere, talented country star —
but a dreamer none the less. Her own personal
forte, however, is making her dreams come true.
As long as she keeps tapping into her vast reser-
voir of creativity, she remains country music's

most beautifully talented and overwhelmingly successful belle of the ball.

About The Author

Mark Bego is the author of several best-selling books on the music industry, rock & roll, and show business. Heralded in the press as "the Prince of Pop Music Bios," to date — he has written 25 books about the entertainment world. In 1994, in addition to *Country Gals* (Pinnacle Books), Mark is also the author of *Country Hunks* (Contemporary Books), also about the nineties country-music phenomenon.

He has just completed working with Martha Reeves of Martha & The Vandellas, to produce Reeves' autobiography, *Dancing in the Street*. It will be released by Hyperion Books in late 1994.

Mark worked with Micky Dolenz of The Monkees, on Dolenz's 1993 autobiography, *I'm a Believer* (Hyperion Books). A huge critical hit, the book traces Dolenz's life and career from "Circus Boy" in the 1950s, through the three-decade Monkees saga, to his present solo career.

In June of 1992 Harmony Books/Random House

published Mark's biography *Madonna: Blonde Ambition* based on his interviews with Madonna and several of her intimate friends. Swept up into the controversy of Madonna's *Sex* book, Mark has appeared on several national television talk shows, discussing his book, and the whole Madonna phenomenon. In 1992 he was seen on "The Joan Rivers Show," "Maury Povich," "Hard Copy," "Faith Daniels" and "Entertainment Tonight." Bego is also the host of the 1993 hour-long biographical videocassette entitled "Madonna: The Name Of The Game" (Brentwood Video). In Hong Kong in the summer of 1993, "Madonna: The Name Of The Game" was broadcast as a television special.

In 1991 Mark Bego published his collaboration with Jimmy Greenspoon of Three Dog Night, *One Is the Loneliest Number* (Pharos Books), and worked with Vanilla Ice to write *Ice Ice Ice: The Extraordinary Vanilla Ice* (Dell).

In 1989, Bego paired with teenage singing star Debbie Gibson, and together they wrote her biographical book, *Between The Lines* (1989). His Michael Jackson biography, *Michael!* (1984), spent six weeks on *The New York Times* Best-Seller List, and sold over three million copies in six different languages. His other books have included the biographies *Linda Ronstadt: It's So Easy* (1990), *Aretha Franklin: Queen Of Soul* (1989), *Bette Midler: Outrageously Divine* (1987), *Cher!* (1986), *Whitney!* [Houston] (1986), *Julian Lennon!* (1986), *Sade!* (1986), *Madonna!* (1985), *On The Road With Mi-*

chael! [Jackson] (1984), *The Doobie Brothers* (1980), *Barry Manilow* (1977), and *The Captain & Tennille* (1977).

Bego's books have also encompassed several other entertainment industry subjects. He has written about television: *TV Rock* [The History Of Rock & Roll On Television] (1988) and *The Linda Gray Story* (1988) — and the movies: *The Best Of Modern Screen* (1986) and *Rock Hudson: Public & Private* (1986).

His writing has appeared in numerous magazines including *People, Us, The Star, Celebrity, Cosmopolitan, Penthouse, The Music Connection, Billboard,* and *The National Enquirer.* For two years Mark was the Nightlife Editor of *Cue* magazine in New York City, and from 1983-1985 he was the Editor-In-Chief of *Modern Screen* magazine. In 1992-1993 Bego resumed his magazine editing with "The Complete History Of Madonna" and "The Complete History of Elvis Presley" for Sterlings/MacFadden Magazines. In the November of 1993 issue of *Modern Screen's Country Music Special,* Mark interviewed Billy Ray Cyrus for a cover story on America's number-one country hunk. Frequently he appears on radio and television, talking about the lives and careers of the stars. In 1990 Bego assisted Mary Wilson of The Supremes in editing and writing her autobiographical book *Supreme Faith: Someday We'll Be Together.* Mark Bego divides his time between New York City; Los Angeles; and Tucson, Arizona.

Index